A Child Is Born

COMPLETELY REVISED EDITION

New photographs of life before birth and up-to-date advice for expectant parents

Photographs
Lennart Nilsson

Text
Mirjam Furuhjelm
Axel Ingelman-Sundberg
Claes Wirsén

Drawings
Bernt Forsblad

A Merloyd Lawrence Book
DELACORTE PRESS/SEYMOUR LAWRENCE

Published by
Delacorte Press/Seymour Lawrence
1 Dag Hammarskjold Plaza
New York, New York 10017

Originally published in Swedish under the title *Ett barn blir till* by Albert Bonniers Förlag. Copyright© 1965 by Albert Bonniers Förlag, Stockholm. Revised edition copyright© 1976 by Lennart Nilsson, Mirjam Furuhjelm, Axel Ingelman-Sundberg, Claes Wirsén.

English translation copyright© 1966, 1977 by Dell Publishing Co., Inc.

Manufactured in the United States of America

Layout by Per Olov Larsson

20   19   18   17

Library of Congress Cataloging in Publication Data
Main entry under title:

A Child is born.

    Translation of Ett barn blir till.
    First English ed. entered under L. Nilsson.
    Includes index.
    1. Pregnancy.   2. Childbirth.   I. Nilsson,
Lennart, 1922–   II. Nilsson, Lennart,
1922–   Ett barn blir till.   English.
RG525.N5413   1977   612.6'3   77–8364

ISBN 0-385-28136-6 (previously ISBN 0-440-01266-X)

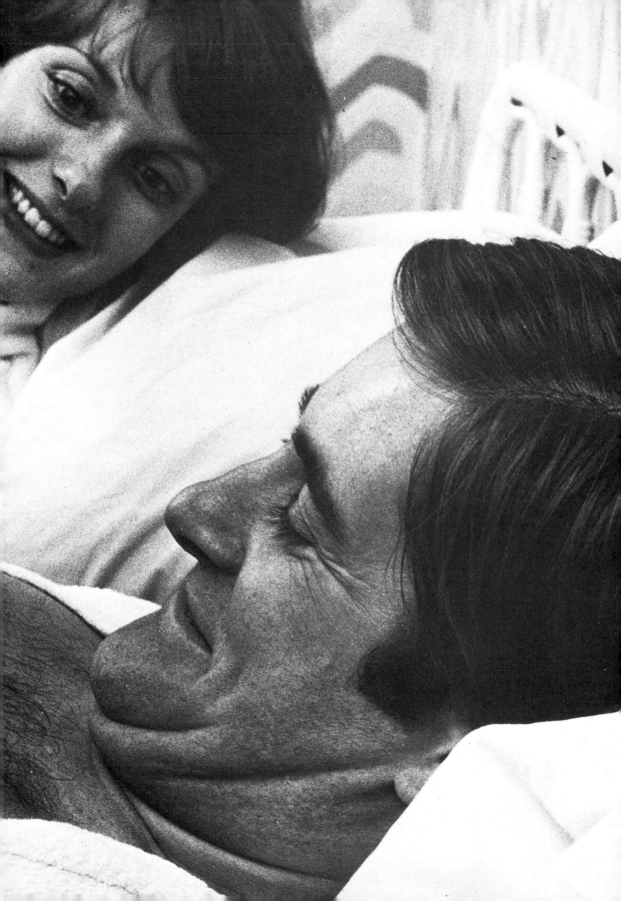

LENNART NILSSON is a pioneer in the field of scientific medical photography. In recognition of his work, he was recently promoted to Doctor of Medicine (Hon.) at Stockholm University. He works in cooperation with several scientists in Sweden and abroad, and by means of his special equipment has contributed to their research as well as recording it. In cooperation with optical instrument manufacturers, he has developed special devices making possible, for example, the reproduction of objects in very small cavities with previously unattainable depth of field. Photos taken with such a lens system are published for the first time in this book, on pages 116–117 and 120–121. He has also used the scanning electron microscope to reproduce surfaces in large-scale enlargement with great depth of field. These pictures have been published in international scientific periodicals. Since the first appearance of this book, in 1965, Lennart Nilsson has widened his field of work to cover the entire body. In 1973 *Behold Man* was published, a unique pictorial documentation of the workings and structure of the human body. Human reproduction, however, continues to be of special interest to him.

MIRJAM FURUHJELM, M.D., is Senior Lecturer and Assistant Chief Physician at the same hospital as her husband, Axel Ingelman-Sundberg. The two have collaborated on the sections of this book about the expectant mother-to-be. Their practical advice on pregnancy is thus based on extraordinarily rich experience.
AXEL INGELMAN-SUNDBERG, M.D., is Professor at the Karolinska Institute and Chief Physician at the women's clinic of Sabbatsbergs Hospital. Thanks to him, Lennart Nilsson had the opportunity to take most of the pictures in this book. As one of Sweden's most prominent and well-known specialists in women's diseases, with an international practice as well, he has been consulted by innumerable pregnant women.

CLAES WIRSÉN, M.D., Senior Lecturer at the Karolinska Institute, has conveyed the fundamentals of embryology to many future doctors and dentists. Through the Swedish TV film *That's How Life Begins*—also based on Lennart Nilsson's photographs—he gradually began to work as a producer, and he is now responsible for the medical programs on Channel 1 of Swedish television. In this book, he wrote the sections explaining prenatal development, and together with Lennart Nilsson he selected the photographs, from the thousands taken by Nilsson.

Contents

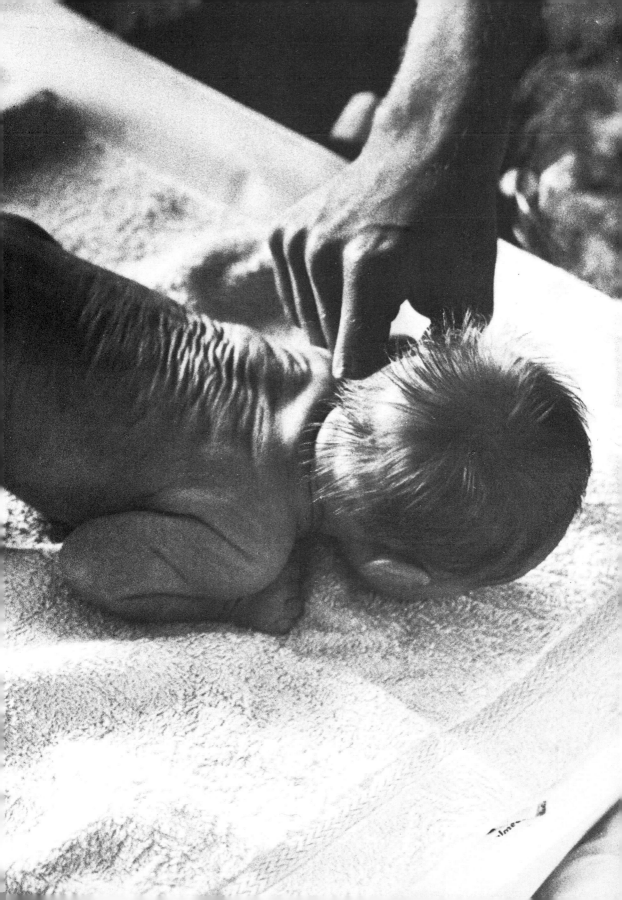

PREFACE AND ACKNOWLEDGMENTS

The revolution that occurs in a young woman's body when she becomes pregnant might be compared with another explosion of life force: the rising of sap in the spring. A woman who was thin and lean now blossoms and, within a few months' time, develops physically into a fully matured woman. How this happens, how the fetus and the placenta are developed, and how various problems and complications should be met have already been described in a great number of books. But so far no book published can be compared to this one. Here, parents-to-be can actually follow and study the wonder which is taking place inside the woman, week by week.

The photographs presented by Lennart Nilsson, after many years of hard work in cooperation with a number of Swedish clinics, are unique and give a picture of human development from the moment of conception until birth that is artistic as well as accurate. Step by step, readers can follow the different stages of fetal growth. They learn when the different organs are formed, when the heart begins to beat, when the small arms and legs begin to move, etc. The new life taking shape inside the mother-to-be thus becomes vivid and more easily recognizable as a new and independent individual.

Lennart Nilsson's clear and easily comprehended picture of human life in the womb is intended not only for expectant parents, but for other readers of all ages. This new, revised edition gives a still richer picture of an extraordinary phenomenon: A child is born.

—Mirjam Furuhjelm,
Axel Ingelman-Sundberg

Our knowledge of human fetal development has always been based largely on observations made when a pregnancy, for one or another reason, is interrupted. This information is not easily gained. Years of patient waiting, day and night, for the right opportunities, combined with highly developed technical skill in the few precious minutes when photographs can be taken, lie behind a work of this kind. The epoch-making importance of Lennart Nilsson's achievements lies in the unique clarity and sharpness of detail with which he reveals the prenatal existence of man. For the first time, people outside of research laboratories are able to share this knowledge.

Ten or fifteen years ago, Lennart Nilsson was the pioneer in this field. During recent years he has cooperated with several scientists and made use of advanced technical methods, such as the scanning electron microscope, with its entirely new pictorial effects.

New pictures, new scientific achievements, new generations of readers—this also means a new opportunity, a new challenge. Consequently, a new book now replaces this ten-year-old classic. At the time of the first edition I was making my first attempts as a popular scientific writer; today I present medical facts to a wide public. As a general medical TV producer, however, I have not been able to keep in constant touch with developments in my old speciality: embryology. I am therefore very happy that a number of my medical colleagues have gone through the new text, checking that the data agree with the latest research. I would especially like to express my thanks to Dr. Gösta Jonsson, Senior Lecturer at the Institution of Histology, Karolinska Institutet, Professor Ove Nilsson, the Biomedical Center at Uppsala University, Professor Jan Lindsten, the Laboratory of Clinical Genetics at Karolinska Hospital, Dr. Margareta Eriksson, Senior Lecturer, the Children's Medical Clinic at St. Görans Hospital, Stockholm, and Dr. Kjell Carlström, Senior Lecturer, the Hormone Laboratory at Sabbatsbergs Hospital, Stockholm, for all their valuable advice.

—CLAES WIRSÉN

This book is the result of cooperation with a large number of hospitals and medical-research laboratories, especially in Stockholm and other university cities in Sweden, but also abroad, in several different countries. Without the kindness and the great courtesy I have met from physicians as well as others at these institutions, taking the pictures now presented in this book would never have been possible. Since the book's first edition, the number of those contributing and assisting has increased to such an extent that it would be impossible as well as unfair to mention any names. To all these persons I extend my deeply felt gratitude and appreciation for the help that has been given me so readily and willingly.

—LENNART NILSSON

A child is born

The unborn child is a person no one knows. Will it be a boy or a girl? Will it be dark-haired or blond, tall or short? It has no name and no face. Even the woman who is carrying the child knows only whether it is lively or the quiet, leisurely type. People around her see only a pregnant woman.

The baby just born is a son or a daughter, a person to be given a name and a place in the family. The family itself is born when the gesticulating little bundle is placed in a mother's arms for the first time.

The family just born probably feels a bit bewildered. It is all so new. "So this is our child," the parents think. And if the baby had words to think with, it might think like this: "Well, so this is Mummy and Daddy. They seem kind enough, though clearly they are beginners."

But the whole story does not begin with delivery. The baby has existed for months before—at first signaling its presence only with small outer signs, later on as a somewhat foreign little being which has been growing and gradually affecting the lives of those close by. It is not only the mother-to-be, within whom all this is happening, who has to adapt, but also the prospective father, although everything in his body remains the same as ever. This book explains how a child develops before birth and is born. We hope that parents-to-be will enjoy these months even more if they follow the story from the very beginning.

Cells

All living organisms—plants as well as animals—are built up of cells. The cell is the smallest living building component. Some cells are able to manage by themselves. Bacteria and amoebas, for example, are cells which react to their surroundings, eat, metabolize, and multiply one by one.

These one-celled animals were the first living creatures; not until several cells joined together and divided their tasks among them was it possible for the evolutionary process to direct itself toward higher species. Some cells specialize in motion and become muscle cells, others in feeling and communication, turning into nerve cells, and so on. The assortment of building components is richer in higher animals. In man especially, the nervous system has developed couplings and exclusive features not found in other species. Other than this, the building components in themselves—the types of cells—do not differ much throughout the animal world. And almost all living organisms start up from one single cell: the ferilized ovum, or egg.

One cell becomes two. At far left, the nucleus has already divided into two new nuclei. Next, the newly forming cells bubble and wriggle in order to get free of each other. Finally they achieve complete separation.

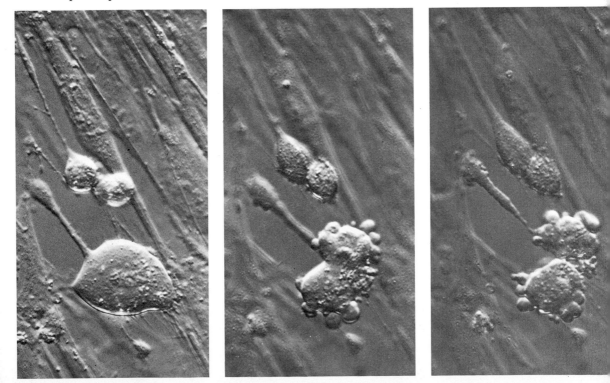

Father

Must there necessarily be a father? Couldn't a cell just come loose now and then and divide and multiply?

Such a solution might not be favorable in the long run. Every normal cell in a living creature contains an exact copy of the genetic material of the first cell with which that creature began. If it were possible to start a human being from one of the later cells, we would simply obtain a duplicate of the original. Mankind would comprise nothing but billions of copies of one and the same individual.

Fortunately, we are different. Our genetic material is derived from two sources. For each one of us, as well as for most of the more-developed animals and plants, life begins with two sex cells. When fusing into one, each contributes half of the genetic material. Living organisms, consequently, can combine their genes. That is why every child resembles its mother as well as its father. The selection of genes differs with each individual (except identical twins). That is why every child resembles its mother and its father in its own special way.

The father thus plays a very important role. He contributes half of the genetic material, half the "blueprint" of the child to be born. But he parts with it. The fusion of the sex cells, as well as the development of the child, takes place outside his body.

Originally the sexes were virtually identical. When living in the sea—as all living beings did some hundred million years ago—females as well as males could shed their sex cells in the surrounding water, where fertilization took place. Terrestrial beings are unable to do this. However, the fusion of the sex cells, or fertilization, must still take place in a medium similar to sea water. Such an environment is found inside the body of the female. Consequently,

in terrestrial animals the sex cells (sperm) of the male must enter the body of the female.

The similarity between the sexes is considerable during the development of the human fetus; in the first months it is virtually impossible to tell the difference between boys and girls. Both possess a pair of rudimentary sex glands with their respective supplies of future sex cells, and the outgoing ducts of each gland in the pair lead to a joint outlet. But the temperature of the body is a couple of degrees too high for sperm production. Therefore, even before birth, the boy's sexual glands, or testicles, will descend into the scrotum—an effective cooling arrangement. At the end of the ducts, other glands are connected; they provide the sperm with a nutritious fluid in which they can swim. Around the outlet a mating organ, or penis, is formed. It is able to stiffen, and thus can be inserted into the woman's body, where the sperm are discharged.

The male reproductive organs

From sexual maturity until an advanced age, the male reproductive apparatus is constantly ready, at short notice, to discharge three to five cubic centimeters of seminal fluid containing several hundred million vigorously swimming sperm. Before the ejaculation, they matured in the epididymis, adjacent to the testicles. Upon sexual excitation the erectile tissue fills with blood, which causes the penis to stiffen, and the sperm are rapidly transported through the spermatic cord to the upper part of the urethra. There the prostate has already left its contribution of substances, which stimulate the uterus as well as the sperm, in order to facilitate the journey of the sperm to the ovum. Finally the seminal vesicles contribute a sugar-containing "fuel." The semen is then ready to be discharged through the urethra by vigorous pumping of the pelvic muscles.

The male reproductive organs
1. penis with erectile tissue
2. left testicle
3. left epididymis
4. left spermatic cord
5. bladder
6. prostate
7. left seminal vesicle

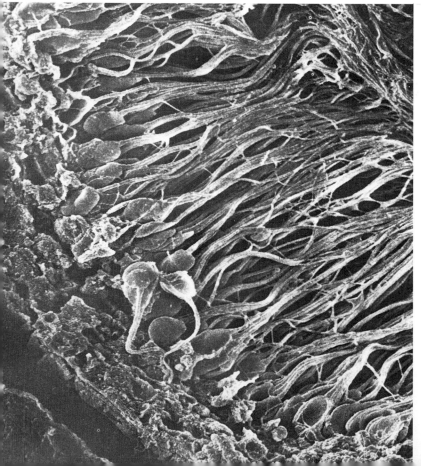

Sperm production magnified a few thousand times by electron microscope. We see a cross section of one of the ducts in the testicle, called *seminiferous tubules*, where the sperm are just ready for discharge. They turn their tails toward the center of the duct. The maturation from sperm-producing cell in the outermost wall layer to fully developed sperm cell takes about two months.

Right: These convolutions all belong to a single duct in the testicle. The total length in both testicles amounts to more than a hundred meters (328 feet).

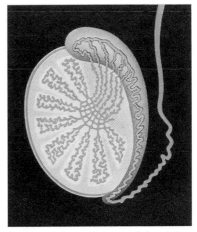

Cross section of a testicle. The testicle is divided into small compartments, each filled up by a tiny convoluted tubule where the sperm cells are produced. Through a series of ducts they are then passed on to the epididymis for maturation. Other parts of the testicular tissue produce the male sex hormone testosterone.

Mother

Most of this story takes place inside the mother-to-be.

Some terrestrial animals—birds, for example—are able to provide their fertilized ova with a protective shell and then lay them. But this means that all the nourishment required for the full development of the fetus must be supplied at the same time. Moreover, the shell must be large enough to contain the young creature until it can manage outside the egg. So far as humans are concerned, this would mean eggs of absurd dimensions.

Mammals present a more elegant solution to the problem, though one that is somewhat more demanding of the mother's body. The eggs themselves are small, roughly the size of the smallest dot visible to the naked eye, 0.13 millimeter (0.005 inch) in diameter. During its very first stage of development, the fertilized ovum obtains nourishment from secretions in the Fallopian tube. After that, it is ready to implant itself in the uterus, eroding the tissue and penetrating the maternal blood vessels so as to gather nourishment for further development. When the fetus has reached full development, it is born, and its connection with the mother's blood system is severed. However, ample provision has been made for a continued supply of nourishment: The mammary glands derive all the necessary substances from the mother's blood and pass them on to the baby through the milk.

Humans seldom give birth to more than one child at a time. The preparation for fertilization and development of this one ovum is far more complicated than the production and discharge of some hundred million sperm.

In both men and women the process is governed by the pituitary gland, a tiny gland located at the base of the brain and itself controlled by the hypothalamus. In the

male, the pituitary gland stimulates the testicular tissue to produce a steady supply of the male sex hormone, which maintains an equally steady supply of sperm. But in the female the interaction between the pituitary gland and the ovaries takes place in four-week rounds. During each round, or *menstrual cycle,* the pituitary gland produces hormones which stimulate the ripening of eggs in the ovary. After about two weeks, one egg has ripened more than the rest and is released from the surface of the ovary. This is called ovulation. Immediately after ovulation the sac or *follicle* in which the ovum developed is transformed into a temporary hormonal gland, producing *progesterone,* a hormone which arrests the ripening of other eggs and prepares the uterine lining to welcome the fertilized ovum. If fertilization does not occur, the lining is shed in menstruation and the whole process starts all over again.

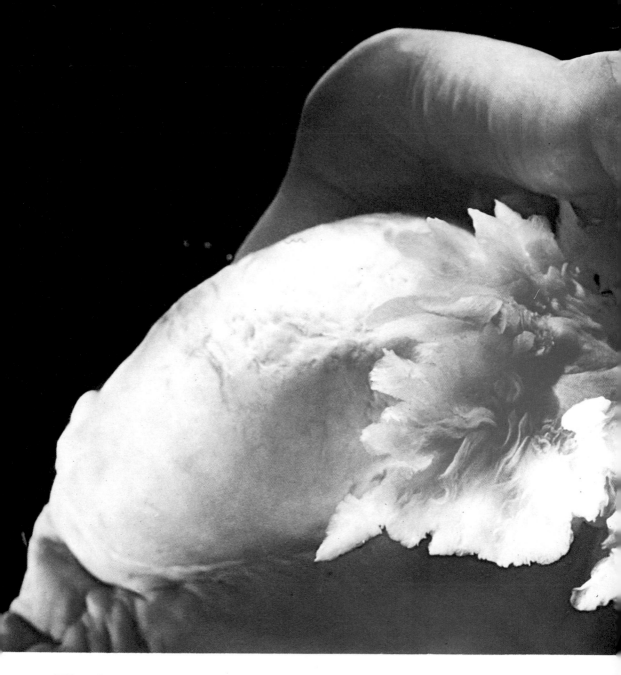

The female reproductive organs

Here we see the funnel-shaped mouth of the Fallopian tube scanning the ovarian surface to catch a mature ovum. In the female there is no system of direct efferent ducts, as in the male. When the ovum is about to mature, it is encased in a sac filled with fluid, the follicle. This follicle rises above the ovarian surface and ruptures. The ovum is then released into the abdominal cavity, but is quickly drawn the right way by the movements of millions of cilia (feathery projections) in the funnel of the Fallopian tube.

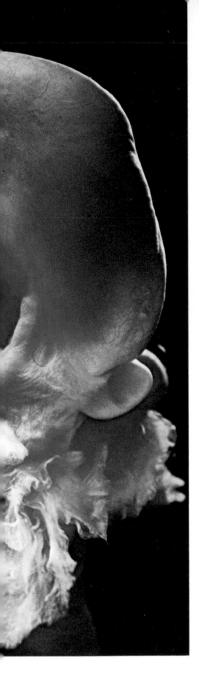

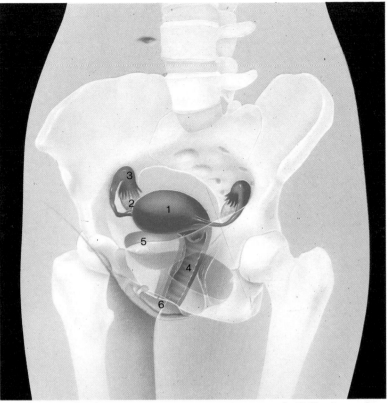

Female reproductive organs   1. uterus, 2. ovary, 3. Fallopian tube, 4. vagina, 5. bladder, 6. labia majora and labia minora on the right side. The vagina is normally flattened, with front and back walls in contact. Thanks to its great elasticity, it adjusts to the penis during sexual intercourse, as well as to the baby's head and shoulders during delivery. The female pelvis is broader and shallower than that of the male, and more open at the bottom. Pelvic measurements can easily be checked by means of X-ray or ultrasound prior to delivery, should any doubts arise.

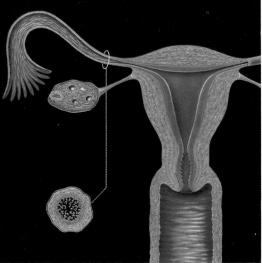

Generally only one follicle a month will mature and rupture. With its thickened walls, the follicle then forms the so-called yellow body, or *corpus luteum*, which secretes progesterone. Here we see a cross section of the Fallopian tube, along which the egg must move.

The Fallopian tube

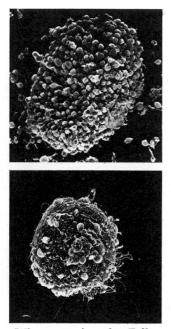

When entering the Fallopian tube, the ovum is embedded in follicle cells (*top*). But these are soon "rinsed" away, so that the protective membrane lies exposed. In the lower photo some follicle cells are still left around the ovum.

The ovum enters the Fallopian tube, which is 10–12 cm (about 4.5 inches) long.

The ovum can be fertilized during an interval of ten to twelve hours, perhaps up to twenty-four hours. If fertilization does not occur, it will disintegrate and be shed along with the uterine lining in the following menstruation.

If there are sperm ready at the right moment, close to the funnel-shaped mouth of the Fallopian tube, the ovum can be fertilized. The ovum will then spend almost all of the first week in this tube, on its way down to the uterus.

The Fallopian tube is quite a remarkable organ. It picks up all ova released from the adjacent ovary. It is able to take care of ova from the opposite ovary as well, if the other Fallopian tube is clogged. It stimulates a large swarm of foreign bodies (sperm) to seek out the ovum; in fact, sperm which have not passed through a uterus and a Fallopian tube are strikingly uninterested in unfertilized ova. The follicle cells, which still surround the ovum when it is released, are loosened by the Fallopian tube to expose the ovum to the sperm. Finally, after fertilization, during the first important days of development, the Fallopian tube meets all the nourishment and environmental requirements of this small, growing community of cells. Hormonal signals from the ovary control the secretion of various useful substances from the large folded surface of the tube throughout the entire menstrual cycle. These signals also control the muscles in the wall of the Fallopian tube as it gently moves the fertilized ovum down toward the uterus. How all this happens we do not entirely know. There are still many riddles here for science to solve.

Actually, it is rather strange that we exist at all. One single ovum, small as the point of a pin, is released into the

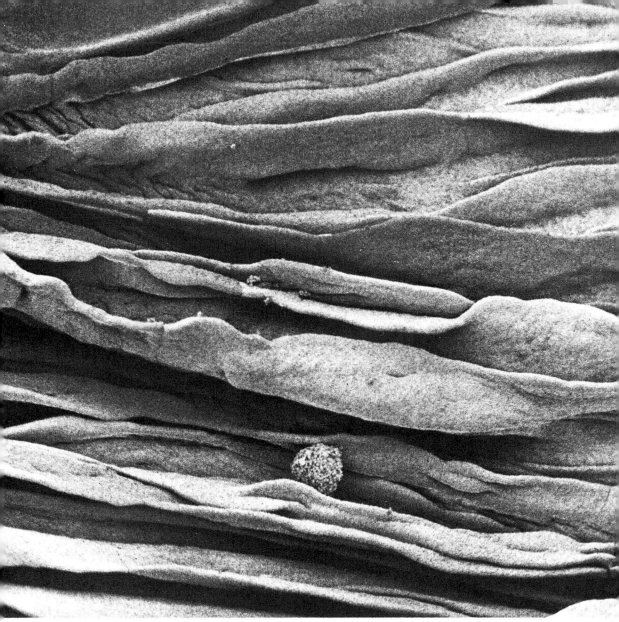

Unfertilized ovum in the folds of the Fallopian tube. Those follicle cells surrounding the ovum at the time of ovulation still remain as an outer envelope. The folded mucous membrane secretes enzymes which gradually cause this cellular envelope to loosen. (Electron microscope, magnified 100 times.)

abdominal cavity every fourth week. What if it were to get lost and fail to enter the Fallopian tube, where the sperm have only hours to find it among all folds and recesses . . . Women do not automatically become pregnant on the first attempt.

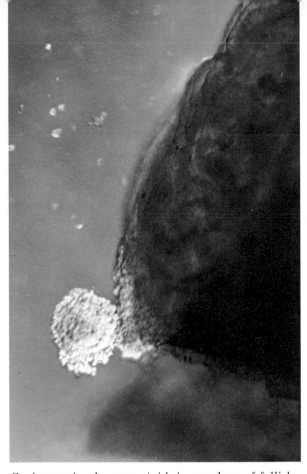

On its way in, the ovum (with its envelope of follicle cells) is just about to disappear behind one of the funnel flaps of the Fallopian tube. Millions of small cilia in this mucous membrane are eagerly flapping toward the interior of the Fallopian tube, and this is one of the reasons why the ovum is sucked in. (Magnified 100 times.)

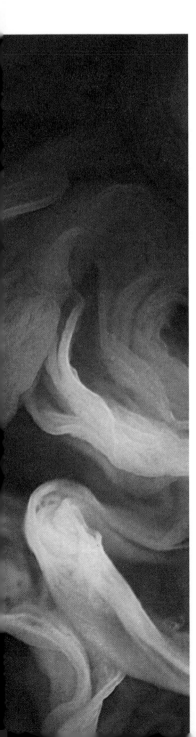

If we were small enough to stand on the ovarian surface just when the follicle ruptured, this is what we would see right above us: the billowing folds of the Fallopian tube, hovering all over the surface in order to pick up the released ovum.

Billions of sperm

Ova and sperm cells are believed to originate from some of the first cells of the body. When the new individual is still a formless mass of a few hundred cells, each of these cells can give rise to any part of the fully developed body; they are not yet specialized. Ova and sperm cells must possess the same versatility if they too, after fusing together, are able to form all kinds of tissues and organs in the new being.

At an early multicellular stage, certain cells are put aside and stored near the place where the sex glands will develop later on. When testicles and ovaries are almost fully developed, these "reserved" cells migrate into the glandular tissue, where they will multiply up to the time of birth.

In the male, this multiplication will continue with the onset of puberty. The pituitary then secretes its sex-gland-stimulating hormones into the blood, and activates those cells in the testicles that produce the male sex hormones. The boy grows into a young man, with coarser body contours, a beard, and a deep voice. The sperm-producing ducts develop and grow. The male will thus have a large store of sperm-producing cells, which all through his life will distribute the genetic material present in the first cells of his body to billions and billions of sperm.

Throughout the testicular duct system we find sperm production in different stages. Fully developed sperm can always be delivered from somewhere. Through two special divisions, the future sex cells have their genetic material divided into halves and mixed. These "great-grandchildren" of the sperm-producing cells are then transformed into fully developed sperm, each with its special blend of hereditary characteristics from the prospective father. Re-

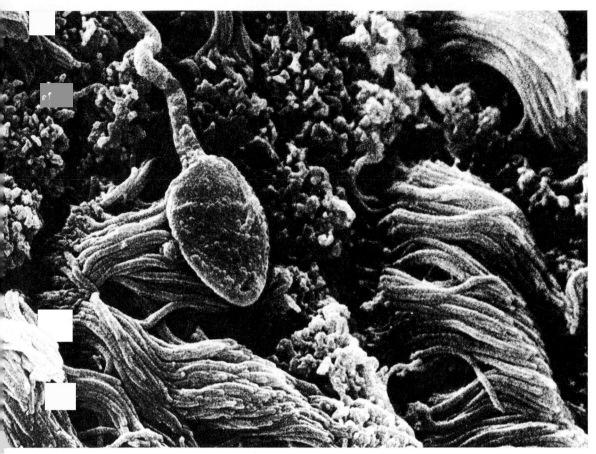

A sperm cell, with its pointed head and long tail. It is on its way to the ovum, and will swim 15–18 cm (6–7 inches)—a journey which will take about six hours.

cently formed sperm then loosen their attachment to the inside of the duct so as to follow the flow to the epididymis for storage and maturation.

Each sperm consists of a small package of concentrated genetic material—the "head"—and a short neck, a middle piece, and a tail, with which it will swim in search of the ovum during the few days it stays alive after ejaculation. It has been calculated that the number of sperm equal to the present population of the earth could easily fit in a thimble. Six or seven good ejaculations would yield a sufficient number.

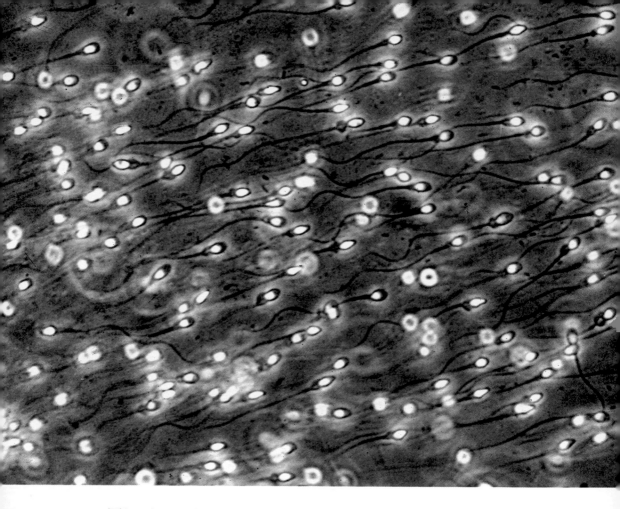

The long journey

Sperm swim together almost in formation. All tails point in the same direction, and all heads are turned forward. These sperm are on their way into the uterus through the protective mucous plug in the cervix, the neck of the uterus. This mucus varies in consistency during different parts of the menstrual cycle. Most of the time it is thick and viscous. Around the fourteenth day of the menstrual cycle, when the ovum is to enter the Fallopian tube, the mucus is clear as glass, and half liquid. Its molecules then stretch out in a pattern that allows the sperm to pass between them, farther on into the uterus.

Sperm which do not arrive at this time are less fortunate. It is difficult for them to penetrate the viscous mass of entangled mucous molecules, which present an effective barrier to sperm during most of the menstrual cycle.

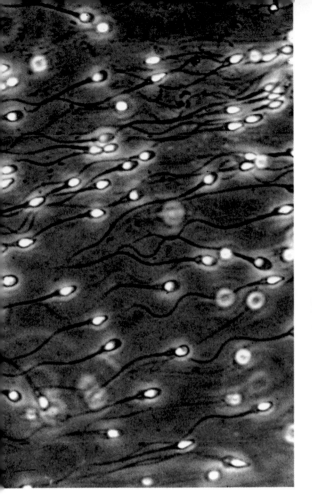

Sperm in cervical mucus on the fourteenth day of the menstrual cycle. We can easily distinguish the oval, slightly pointed head, the short body, and the whiplash tail. (Magnified about 450 times.) The length of each sperm cell is approximately 60 microns (0.02 inch).

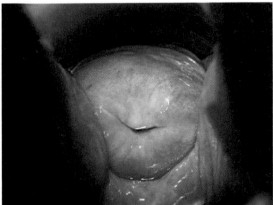

The cervix seen through the vagina. The cervical mucus is like watery jelly—the time is right for fertilization.

Sperm (*left*) are slowly trying to force their way through a viscous drop of mucus at the end of the menstrual cycle. Their ranks will thin out (*middle*), and many will die without having entered (*right*).

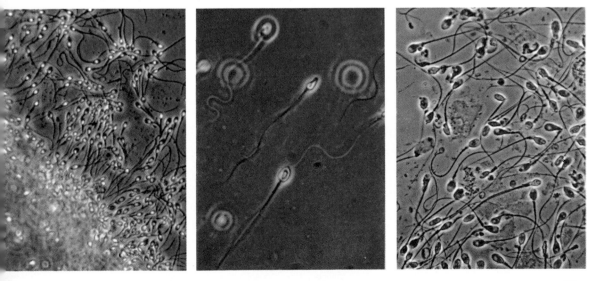

One ovum a month

In view of the enormous mass production of sperm in the testicles of the male, one ovum a month seems rather modest. But one must consider the lengthy preparation involved in building up the uterine lining, and the complicated interaction of hormones triggered off during every menstrual cycle. The million or two primordial egg cells already formed in the female's ovaries at the time of birth are more than sufficient. Assuming roughly 400 menstrual cycles during a woman's fertile years, this means that not even every thousandth primordial egg cell will mature into a fertilizable ovum.

Many of these primordial egg cells succumb even before puberty. During childhood, follicles begin to develop that never reach full maturity. They shrivel up and disappear at an early stage. With the onset of puberty, the girl's pituitary gland secretes the same hormone as does the boy's. Her ovaries then begin to produce the female sex hormones—estrogens—which cause, among other things, the uterine lining to grow and the body to take on female forms.

When there are sufficient quantities of estrogen in the blood, the pituitary gland secretes a hormone that induces one of the follicles to absorb liquid more rapidly than the others, expand, rupture, and release the ovum.

After ovulation the follicle shrinks. Together with the estrogen-producing outer layer, its interior cell layer, which previously surrounded the ovum, now forms the corpus luteum. The corpus luteum is responsible for the other female sex hormone, progesterone, which together with estrogen causes the uterine lining to secrete a nutritious fluid and prepare itself to receive the fertilized ovum with a soft, blood-rich bed.

But the life span of the corpus luteum is limited. About ten days after ovulation, it begins to shrink. After four or five more days, the uterine lining starts to bleed away. Now the pituitary gland secretes follicle-stimulating hormones again. As soon as the old uterine lining is washed away, a new litter of follicles starts developing.

Most of the primordial ova are discarded during the menstrual cycles. Thus, the last primordial ova in the last follicles to respond to the stimulus from the pituitary gland will have been awaiting their turn for more than forty years.

The large cell released from the follicle on the day of ovulation is, strictly speaking, not an ovum but an egg-producing cell, corresponding to the sperm-producing cells in the male. Like these, it undergoes two special divisions to mix and redistribute the genetic material. But does this mean quadruplets? No—the large volume of the egg-producing cell, which makes it a giant among other body cells, is needed to provide material for the first cells of the new being. It is too precious to be divided into four identical parts. The first division, which takes place at ovulation, does not go through the center of the cell but near one of the edges, and results in one large and one small daughter cell. The latter one is called the *polar body,* and can often be seen inside the gelatinous envelope secreted by the surrounding follicle cells to protect the maturing ovum. The next division, which gives rise to the ovum proper plus another polar body, takes place only if a sperm cell arrives.

This cluster of follicle cells around the ovum, which we have seen in earlier photos, appears under the microscope as a beautiful radiant wreath *(corona radiata).* The corona radiata is soon washed away by the Fallopian-tube secretions, but a gelatinous layer remains, which must be penetrated by the sperm themselves. Of course, this slows down the sperm trying to fertilize the ovum. After that, the only barrier is the ovum's own thin cell membrane.

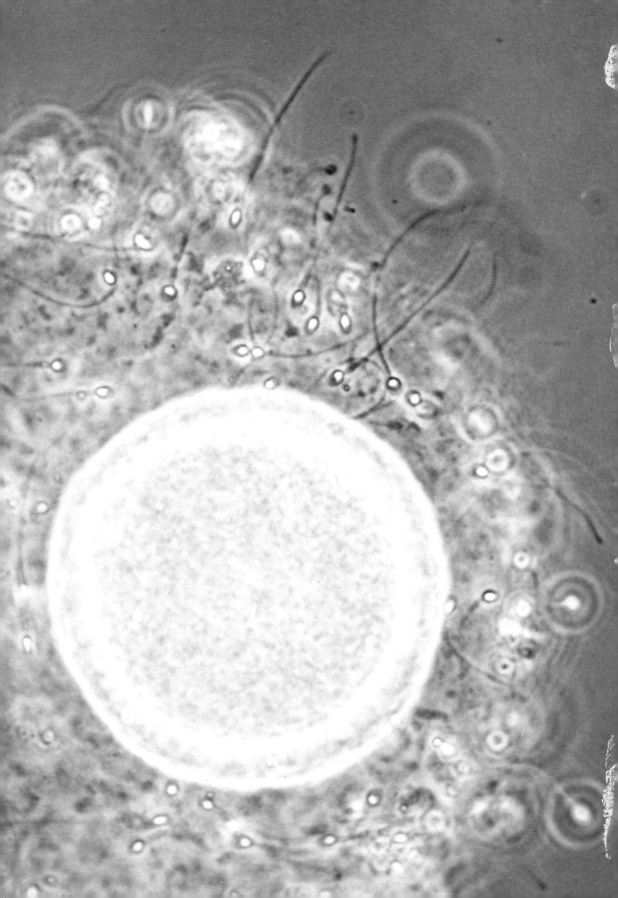

Fertilization

Looking at the large ovum surrounded by the tiny, eager sperm, we can understand the importance of a proper barrier. The first sperm to touch the ovum's cell membrane is well received—it seems as though the ovum assists in drawing it in. But at the same time, a rapid change in the cell membrane sets in, so that the very next sperm (as well as all its comrades) is locked out.

To the left, an ovum ready for release has been extracted and put into a nutritive solution together with a drop of specially treated seminal fluid. The sperm are eagerly striving toward ovum. Notice the difference in size.

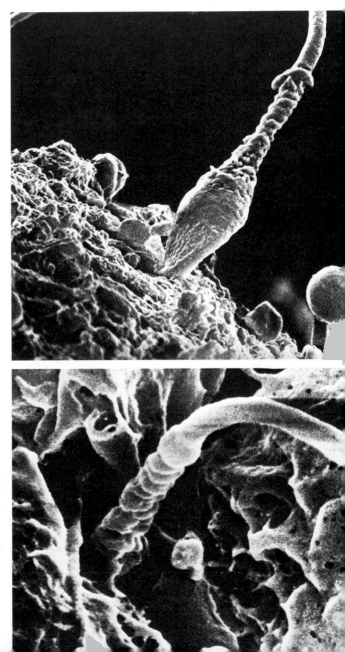

To the right, two electron-microscope pictures. A sperm has just touched the surface of the ovum, and another has obviously entered with its head. When the sperm is completely submerged in the ovum it dissolves, and the genetic material is set free. The genes of the future parents meet for the first time.

Chromosomes

In the nucleus of the cell, the genes are very neatly lined up along the thin, spiraled molecule threads which constitute the framework of the chromosomes.

When a cell is at work, the spirals lie stretched out inside the nucleus—the "order center" of the cell—and are almost impossible to detect even when greatly magnified. But when the cell is about to divide, they are strongly contracted, and it is then possible, with the help of a microscope, to see clearly what the chromosomes look like.

Each chromosome consists of two identical halves held together at a single point somewhere between the ends. With their halves standing slightly apart, many of the chromosomes look like X's, with "arms" and "legs" of varying length. During cell division, the X's are split lengthwise, so that each daughter cell will have its own half. A new "arm" and a new "leg" are then formed through duplication. The X's are complete again and can take part in subsequent divisions.

Through this ingenious duplication mechanism, the same line of genes is handed over from generation to generation of new cells. Each of us remains the same individual throughout life, although a great many of the body cells are worn out and replaced by new ones.

Human chromosomes arranged in pairs according to size (*below*). They have been taken from a photo of a cell just about to divide. "Arms" and "legs" have not yet spread apart. The streaky pattern is caused by the coloring used to make the chromosomes show up; it is not equally absorbed along their entire length. First we see the twenty-two "ordinary" pairs. Farthest to the right we see the twenty-third pair—the two X's of equal size (female) and one X and one Y with short arms (male). (*Photo courtesy of the Laboratory of Clinical Genetics, Karolinska Institute*)

Genes are located within the chromosomes and are composed of DNA (deoxyribonucleic acid), the substance by which biological information is transferred. The DNA molecule is the famous double helix, two strands twisted about each other. Along these strands, a kind of chemical alphabet, composed of only four letters, is laid out in a sequence which forms the genetic code. After their chemical names, we may call the letters of this alphabet A, C, G, and T.

These letters cannot be combined at random. T suits only A, and G only C. If we have a portion of a line "written" as AGCTTGA, it must be joined like this:

A G C T T G A
T C G A A C T

But this means that one straw, or sequence, determines the other. The halves can be split apart, and new ones built up as exact duplicates of the old ones. And with four "letters," there are ample possibilities for variation. The whole "work plan" of man, in turn, may contain as many as one or two million genes.

Man has forty-six chromosomes, arranged in twenty-three pairs—one in each pair originating from the father, the other from the mother. The twenty-third pair is a bit special; it may contain either two large so-called X chromosomes, or one X and one Y chromosome. This pair decides the sex. XX means girl, and XY means boy. Whether the second chromosome in the pair is an X or a Y is determined by the father's sperm, but the father himself will not know the result until long afterward.

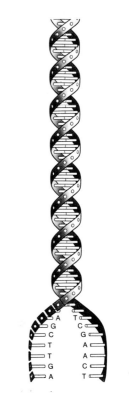

The double helix of DNA. The two strands are matched according to the pattern—A to T, G to C, etc.

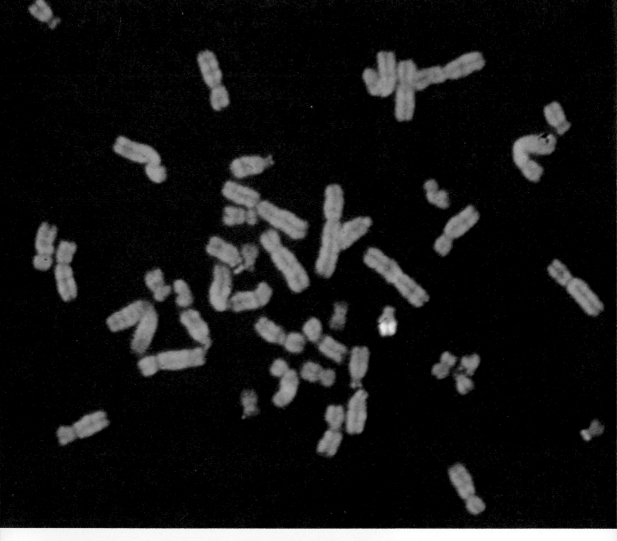

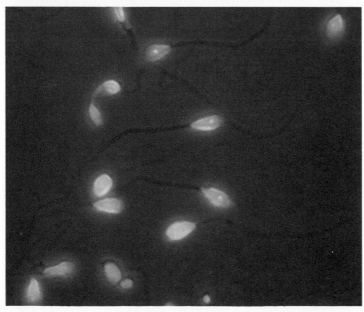

A dividing human cell (*above*) has been flattened out gently so that the chromosomes have floated apart. They have been treated with a substance causing certain parts of them to emit light under ultraviolet rays. Each type of chromosome has its own "pattern." The tiny short-armed Y chromosome (center) emits a particularly strong light.

In sperm (*left*) treated the same way as the chromosomes in the photo above, a small gleaming spot is visible in the "boys." This is the Y chromosome.

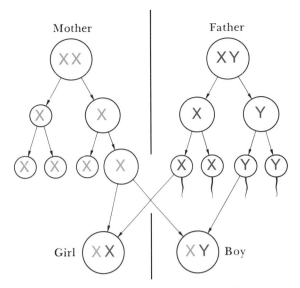

Mother — XX   Father — XY

Girl XX   XY Boy

Determination of sex

In each primordial ovum (above, left) in the mother there are two X chromosomes, and in each primordial sperm (right) there is one X and one Y chromosome—exactly as in the other parts of the body. But when an ovum and a sperm unite upon fertilization, each contributes only half its genetic material. Therefore, the number of chromosomes must be halved when ova and sperm are produced. This division into halves takes place during the two special cell divisions known as *meiosis*.

During these two divisions the chromosome pairs are separated. In the mother, one X migrates to the first little polar body, which cannot give rise to an ovum, and the other goes to the future ovum, which must keep as much cell mass as possible, since it must provide material for the new individual's first cells. In the father the X and Y go to sperm-producing cells of equal size—the sperm will need practically no cell mass at all, and a division into equal parts is therefore possible. When these two divisions have taken place, there will be three small polar bodies and a single fully developed ovum (each with an X, of course) in the mother, and four sperm, two X and two Y sperm, in the father.

At the time of fertilization, all that remains is simple addition:

Ovum (X) + X sperm = XX (girl)
Ovum (X) + Y sperm = XY (boy)

The other twenty-two chromosome pairs go through the same procedure: They are separated and split in two. Consequently, each sperm and each ovum has only one chromosome of each type.

But prior to the separation, the chromosomes in each pair (except for X and Y, which do not fit well together) place themselves close to each other, full length, and exchange long sequences of genes. This exchange leads to different results for every ovum to be produced in the mother, and for every fourth sperm in the father. That is why the boy and the girl resemble their parents, but each in his or her special way.

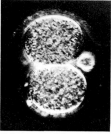

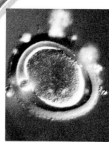

Inside the protective gelatinous envelope, the first polar body is pinched off.

After roughly twenty-four hours the fertilized ovum divides. The first two cells come into existence. One of the two polar bodies is visible.

The division of cells continues. Soon they will have reached normal cell size.

Within the ovary we see the development of the follicle (counterclockwise) from a thin cellular layer surrounding the future ovum to corpus luteum. (It does not actually move around.) After implantation, the corpus luteum does not shrink; the progesterone it secretes maintains the uterine lining.

The first week

Around the fourteenth day of the menstrual cycle, the ovum is released from the follicle, picked up by the Fallopian tube, and, if a sperm is there at the right time, fertilized. This picture represents one ovum in different stages of development. The new individual spends its first days gradually moving through the Fallopian tube, while its cells are multiplying. When passing into the uterus, it is a tiny "human seed" inside a vesicle (sphere) of cells. These cells eat their way into the uterine lining for shelter and nourishment. This is called *implantation*. When the vesicle lands, there is one week left until the following menstruation—which must be prevented if the future being is to develop.

When the fertilized ovum is passed into the uterus (*right*), the rapidly growing external cells form a sphere which will gradually push off the gelatinous envelope. Direct contact with the mucous membrane of the uterus is now possible. The internal cells —the "human seed"—are biding their time.

The vesicle (*right*) has landed between two gland orifices. The outer cells are multiplying and invading the mucous lining to reach the dilated blood vessels. The "seed" has turned into a disc with two cell layers: the first germ layers.

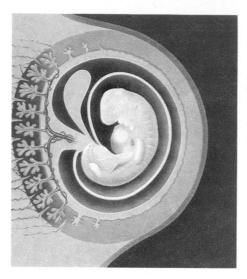

After the third week it is easy to recognize what is what. The embryo has a body with a head and a tail. It swims in the fluid inside the amniotic sac. The yolk sac can be seen next to the body stem. The first blood vessels are developing in the primitive placenta (*left*).

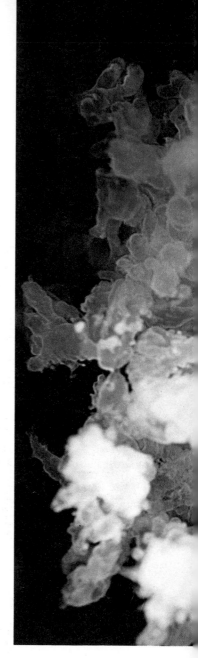

Shelter and nourishment

During the first two days of the second week, the vesicle digs its way down, and ends up completely submerged in the uterine lining. The outer cells multiply rapidly while penetrating an increasing number of blood vessels. The woman's blood now flows freely through a thick, spongy layer of cells, which absorbs nourishment for the "human seed": the embryo. A primitive placenta has taken shape. The side of the vesicle facing away from the uterine wall has become a smooth surface: the outer fetal membrane, or *chorion*.

Once shelter and nourishment have been established, the "human seed" begins to grow in earnest. Over its two-layered disc another cavity develops, which will become the amniotic sac. The disc then starts to curve and expand, and becomes a rounder body with a head and a tail end, attached to the placenta by a stem, the future umbilical cord. The lower layer begins to change into a primitive intestine with a funny protuberance, the yolk sac, similar to that of a fish embryo. An intermediate layer has also formed, where a primitive system of blood circulation is developing.

Menstruation is now one week overdue, and the mother-to-be begins to wonder.

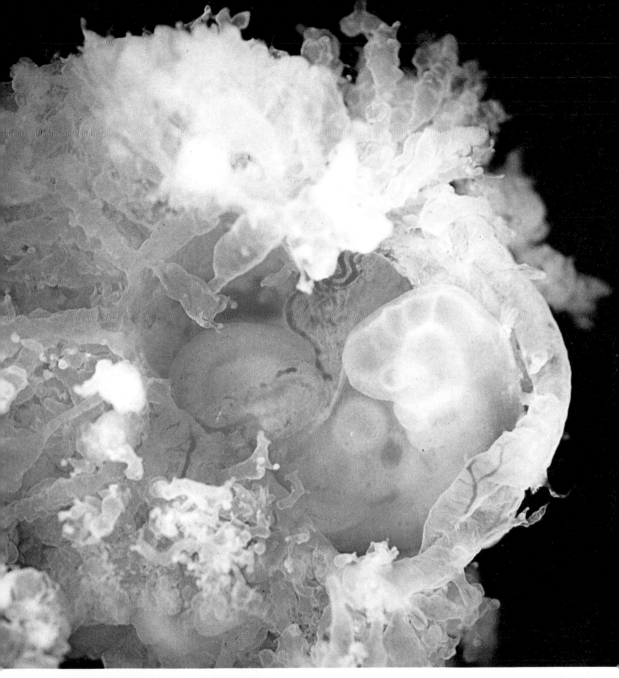

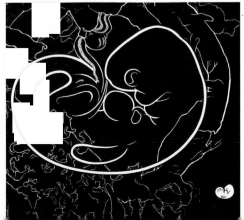

At 4–5 weeks, 7–8 mm (0.3 inch). Here the chorion and amniotic sac have been opened so that we can see the little embryo. In the head end there is an indication of the future eye. Along the side of the trunk the left arm and leg buds are also visible. The outside of the chorion is shaggy, which increases the area absorbing nourishment. In the drawing the little white figure at bottom right shows the actual size of the embryo at this time.

Pregnancy test

"Am I pregnant?"

With conventional tests the question cannot be answered until ten to fourteen days after menstruation should have come. The embryo is then in its fourth week. The primitive heart has started to beat. The new being does not look especially human yet, but the general outlines of a body with a head and a trunk and extremities can be made out. Pregnancy tests are designed to detect the first faint hormonal signals from the placenta.

When the embryonic vesicle is first implanted, its situation is quite precarious. When fertilization does not occur, the corpus luteum begins to shrivel, and in another few days the uterine lining is shed in the next menstruation. But after implantation, this does not happen. The initiative in the hormonal interaction is now taken over by the placenta and the developing embryo. Special cells in the chorionic tissue, now part of the placenta, send a hormone through the woman's blood, a hormone much the same as the one secreted by the pituitary gland to trigger off the activity of the corpus luteum. The corpus luteum continues its activity, and the uterine lining remains. No menstrual period occurs.

Like many other hormones, this placental hormone, which is called *human chorionic gonadotropin* (HCG), is excreted through the kidneys. The urine can thus be tested to determine its presence. A urine sample is first mixed with a solution containing antibodies against HCG. To this mixture is added a suspension of red blood cells (or latex particles) coated with HCG. In a negative sample the antibodies react with the HCG-coating, and the blood cells or the particles clot and clump together. But if HCG is already present in the urine sample—as during preg-

A small urine sample to which the antibody solution has been added is pipetted into a test tube with a suspension of HCG-coated red blood cells. After one or two hours, the result can be seen in the light of the examination stand: left, a positive sample, where the blood cells have sunk into a ring, indicating pregnancy; right, a negative sample, with clotted blood cells floating in the urine and thus not visible.

nancy—the antibodies react with the HCG instead. If the HCG content is high enough, no antibodies are left to cause clotting. Therefore, in a positive sample, the red blood cells or latex particles float freely, and sink to the bottom of the test tube to form a clearly defined ring.

The neural tube

The nervous system starts developing at the end of the third week after fertilization. The outer germ layer—the "skin" of the embryo—thickens along a central line and simultaneously lifts into two longitudinal folds. This results in a groove leading from front to rear. The groove closes to form a tube as the folds meet and fuse, beginning from the "waist" and continuing out toward the ends. The top of the tube then swells to form a brain, and nerve fibers begin to grow out from the brain and the primitive spinal cord.

At 4 weeks, about 6 mm (just under 0.25 inch). The embryo's back is turned toward us. The neural groove is closed almost completely; at the top the cleft still shows. Arm buds bulge out to each side. The yolk sac is seen to the left of the body. In human beings it serves only as a blood-cell factory and does not contain any reserve nourishment.

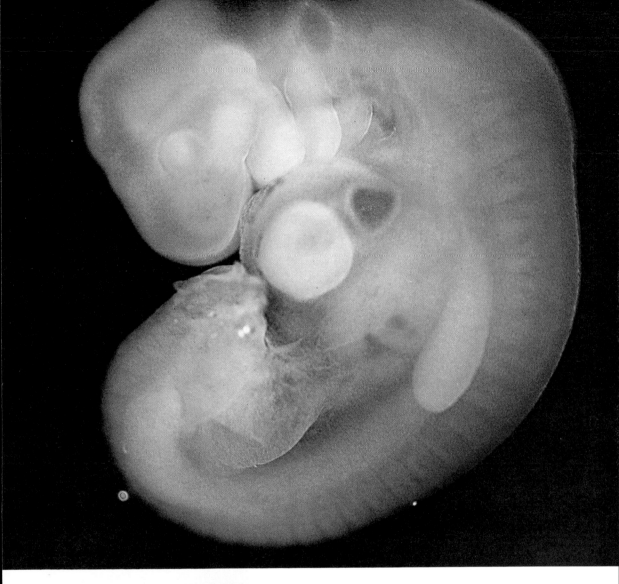

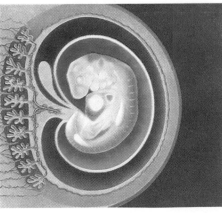

At 4 weeks, about 7 mm (0.3 inch). The embryo now has a body with a head, a trunk, and a tail. It almost literally has its heart in its mouth. The "double chins" are known as branchial (gill) arches, features which we have in common with all vertebrates at this stage. On the side of the trunk, an arm bud and a leg bud bulge out.

A body takes shape

Not yet a cute baby, this little embryo is now entering its fourth week. A blunt head end projects forward, with a large primitive mouth opening just above the heart. The body ends in a pointed tail. Now arms and legs, brain and nervous system, backbone and face will begin to develop.

The body wall now consists of three layers—the two primary germ layers have one more between them. The outer layer will later on give rise to the epidermis, with hair, sebaceous glands, and sweat glands; its first task is to establish a nervous system with a brain and a spinal cord. From the middle layer there will emerge the deeper layer of the skin, the dermis and subcutaneous tissue, muscles, skeleton, blood vessels, and lymph glands, kidneys and sex glands, and connective tissue and blood cells. At this point, the middle layer has already built up a primitive blood circulation with a simple one-chambered heart, and next it will produce a backbone. The innermost layer has formed a primitive intestinal tube, which will be provided with mucous membranes and glands; lungs will bud out from the upper part, the urinary tract from below.

During this fourth week, the fact that we are vertebrates begins to appear. On each side of the neural groove, exactly where it is closing, paired blocks of tissue called *somites* begin to develop. The total number of these pairs will exceed forty, right out to the tip of the tail. Thirty-two or thirty-three of these become vertebrae, while the tail regresses and finally disappears. Muscle primordia form, leading from vertebra to vertebra as well as between the ribs, which begin to grow out from the twelve primordial thoracic vertebrae. Between the vertebrae, nerve stems are growing out from the developing spinal cord.

Between the primitive mouth and the heart, the future

face and neck begin to take shape. From both sides six projections grow out, bending toward the center, where they meet and fuse to form arches. It looks as though the baby were going to have gills. The top arch gives rise to the lower jaw. A cleft chin shows where the fusion took place. This rapid and complex development requires an effective supply of nourishment. The placenta grows deep into the blood-filled spaces in the uterine lining. This creates an ever-increasing area of absorption, through which nourishment from the woman's blood is forwarded into the embryo's developing circulation.

At 4 weeks, about 7 mm (0.3 inch). The gill arches will soon close. Behind the second arch from the top the future heart is showing. The somites now extend in a row right out to the tip of the tail.

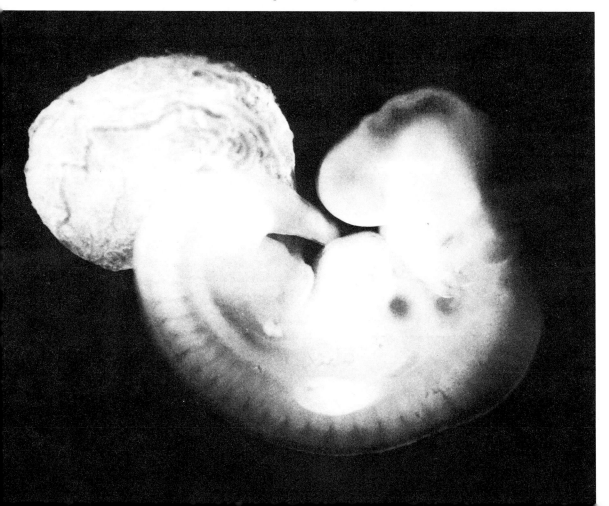

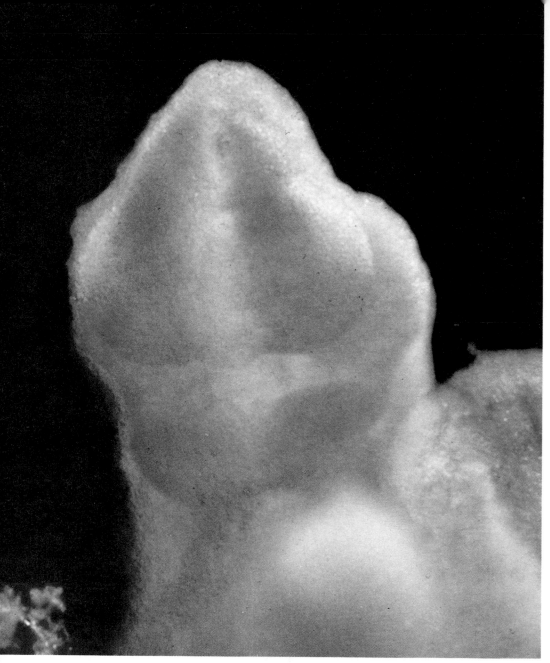

At 26 days, 3 mm (0.12 inch). The earliest portrait of a human being at the embryo stage. The hole in the middle of the forehead is the front opening of the neural tube, which is just about to close, and the arch of the lower jaw is joined just below the pale mouth opening. The cheeks begin to form. Eyes are still missing. The bulging below the chin in the foreground is the heart. It started to beat a few days earlier.

About 4 weeks, 5 mm (0.2 inch). Eye and ear begin to show. The head and neck are half the body length; the shoulders will be located where the whitish arm buds are attached. ▶

An unknown being

At first the embryo has no face at all—no human features whatsoever. The fertilized egg of a sea urchin is deceptively similar to that of man. All multicellular beings start from a small, primitive cluster of cells. It takes time until it is possible even to guess where in the animal kingdom the future individual will end up. Facial characteristics do not begin to show until late in fetal development.

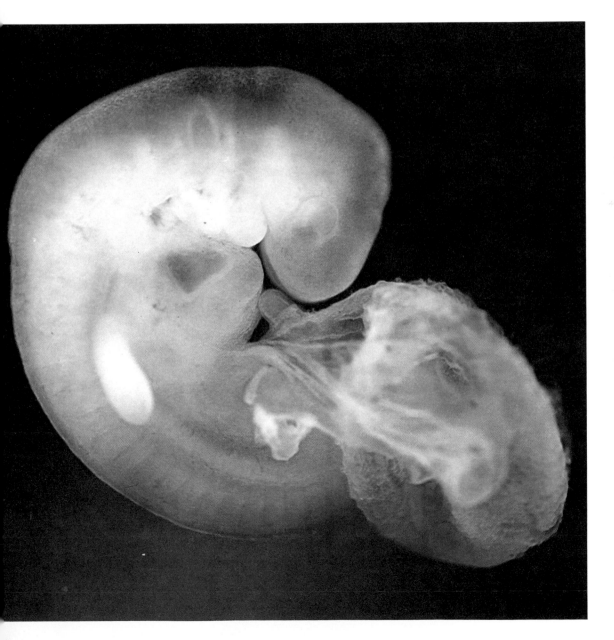

The embryo–fish
or fowl?

Around the thirtieth day of its life, the embryo has become about 6–7 mm long (0.25 inch), and begins to resemble a vertebrate. But not even a loving mother would think that it resembles its parents.

Now development progresses very rapidly. The child-to-be grows a whole millimeter a day (0.04 inch). The heart pumps increasing quantities of blood through a vessel system which forms a rich network in all the placental outgrowths, like the root system of a tree. The chorionic sac expands, pressing the uterine lining upward more and more, and the placenta continues to spread.

It is often said that individual development reflects that of the whole species. We all start as one-celled beings. Eggs and sperm of the sea urchin are, at a hasty glance, very similar to those of man. A fish embryo swims around with a yolk sac under its belly, and also has six gill arches between the mouth and the heart. Nor is the difference between the chicken in the egg and the human embryo in the chorionic sac so very great on the day of the first heartbeat, though the chicken needs only two days to get to that point. When is it determined that we are going to be human beings?

This happens at the moment of conception. Certainly we have much in common with other species, especially during early stages, related as we are. But for each species, growth is staked out from the beginning. Human genetic material can give rise only to human beings. The similarity between the human embryo and the fish embryo consists in the fact that they both, being vertebrates, develop the same primitive features. But they make different uses

At 30 days, 6–7 mm (0.24–0.28 inch). Chick, fish embryo, rabbit embryo, or human being? The scientists who first began to study the early stages of development found to their amazement that more unites the species than separates them. Darwin's teachings about the origin of the species received early support from the studies of the development of embryos (comparative embryology). Nowadays evolutionary theory has been supplied with still more evidence thanks to the research done on the molecules of the genetic material and their structure.

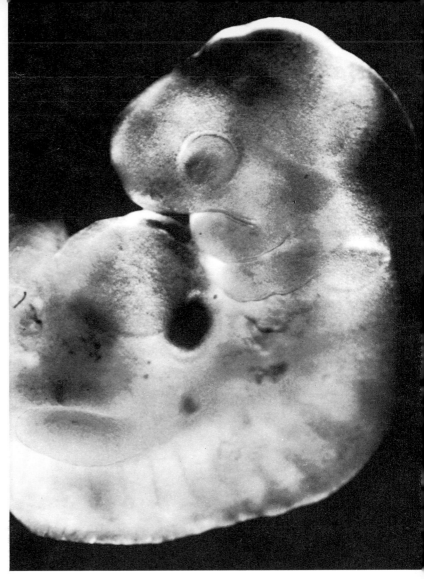

of them. The fish embryo, developing outside its mother, carries its nourishment supply in the yolk sac. The human embryo, as we said before, uses the yolk sac as a blood-cell factory. Fish make gills out of their four inferior gill arches. We make a lower jaw, a tongue bone (hyoid bone), and a larynx out of our six arches. How we and other higher vertebrates once evolved from amoebas, fishes, and reptiles —that is a different story.

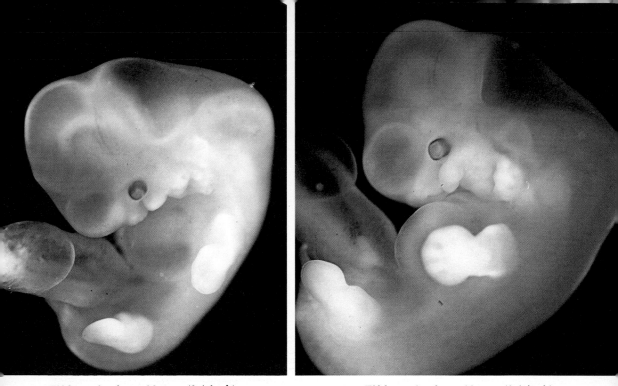

Fifth week, about 10 mm (0.4 inch). The head is bent down toward the bulging skin of the chest, covering the heart. Arms and legs are still nothing but rounded buds.

Fifth week, about 10 mm (0.4 inch). The nose and the cheeks begin to show under the eyes. What looks like a wavy mouth is the future outer ear.

The fifth week

In the fifth week, face, trunk, and extremities are growing. The head begins to straighten up from its bent position. Arm and leg buds are no longer simply bulges; one can see that they are going to be a hand and a foot. But arms and legs are still short round stalks.

The front end of the neural tube develops into a brain. For the time being there is only a pair of vesicles farthest to the front, and three in a row behind them. The pair in the front is the future cerebrum, with its two halves. The brain vesicles are clearly visible through the delicate skin. There are no skull bones yet.

The head end is still the largest part, and the arms have developed further than the legs. This is how we develop, from the head downward. We learn to grasp before we are able to walk.

End of fifth week, 11–12 mm (0.43–0.47 inch). The head is more erect. Five fingers are faintly visible. The body stem has become an umbilical cord. ▶

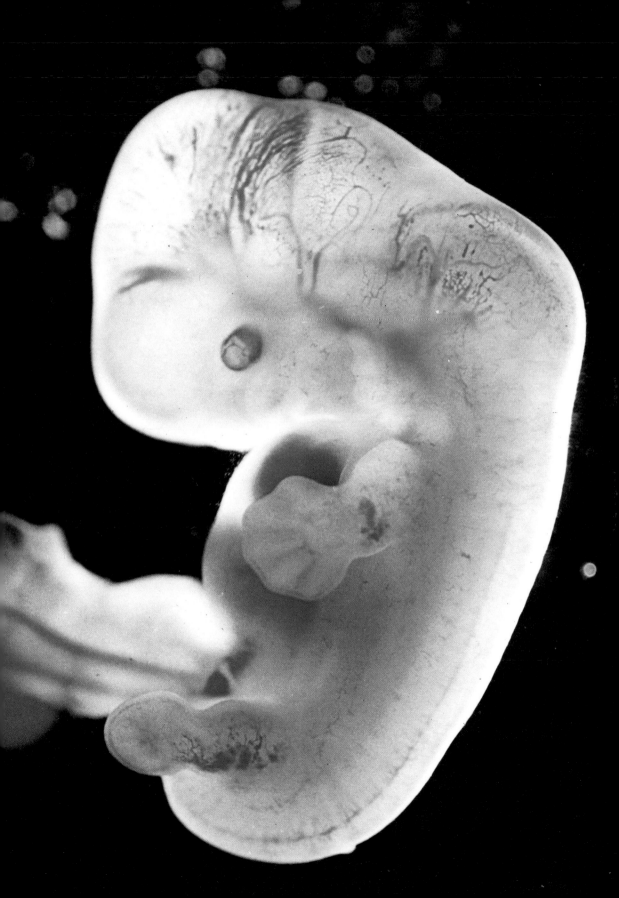

The work plan

In each of his or her cells, there is a complete "work plan" for the human being. This work plan is strictly personal. It consists of the specific combination of gene sequences which has been conveyed to this individual from his or her parents.

But only the details vary, never the fundamental pattern. Through the ingenious copying mechanism of the DNA, this fundamental pattern will be handed over from generation to generation. No matter what happens to the individual, man will remain a species so long as new children are born and live until they can reproduce and pass on the genetic code.

Now, if every cell has the same work plan, how can we explain the fact that so many different kinds of cells are formed? We have seen that the single fertilized ovum develops into germ layers, placenta, and fetal membranes. And out of the germ layers, a whole assortment of different tissues takes shape: the embryo. The explanation is not so strange—in principle, that is, since we do not know how this really comes about. But it might be put like this: At a building site, everybody may have access to the blueprints or working drawings but still not perform more than his own part of the work.

Brown eyes and dark hair, for example, are inherited. This does not mean that all the child's cells will have brown eyes and dark hair—this information concerns only the pigment cells of the iris and the hair follicles. All the other cells also have these genes, but they do not use them. At every step of the way to a fully developed human being, we can observe that different cells choose their part from the blueprint and keep to that part only. Consequently, we do not get millions of copies of the ovum, but a highly organized society of cells, in which each group has been given its own specific task.

But the fertilized ovum is not specialized—otherwise it would not be able to give rise to a complete human being. Nor are the first cells inside the gelatinous envelope in the Fallopian tube. Separated from each other, each of them is still able to build up a vesicle with a "human seed" in it. And if there should be two "seeds" in that one ovular vesicle, we would then have two developing embryos, though they would then have to share the same placenta and perhaps even a common inner fetal membrane. This is how identical twins come about—twins or more. Fraternal twins, on the other hand, are only siblings of the same age, who happen to develop during the same pregnancy because more than one ovum was released from the ovaries.

Identical twins are identical. They have the same genetic code, and could actually be regarded as duplicates of each other. Consequently, they can quite easily give blood to each other, and it is also possible to transplant organs or tissues from one to the other without the recipient's rejecting them.

This has to do with the fact that the work plan is so strictly personal. Identical twins are, so to speak, the same person, but the rest of us are not. The proteins which are each individual's signature (on the outside of the cells) are specific to him or her. During the later stages of fetal development, when the immune system develops resistance against foreign intruders, certain cells have to learn, "This is *me*. This is the protein pattern of *my* body." The organism does not turn against itself so long as that protein pattern can be recognized.

Cells which are specialized do not always start their work at once. The body has the capacity to create new cells which take over as soon as they are needed. That is what happens when a wound is healing and new skin is made. That is what happens in the bone marrow, where new blood cells are constantly produced to replace those dying away, and in the intestinal mucous membrane, where the working cells of the surface have a life span of only a couple of days.

Nothing is complete in the fetal stage—it is only the beginning.

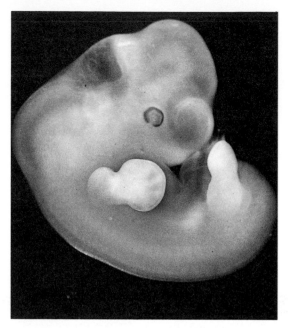

At 5–6 weeks, 10–12 mm (0.43–0.47 inch). The cerebrum makes a curve in the forehead. The brain stem grows so long that it has to fold in order to find space—one curve upward above the eye and another, smaller bend downward in the neck. The hands show faint signs of fingers, but the foot still looks like a paddle.

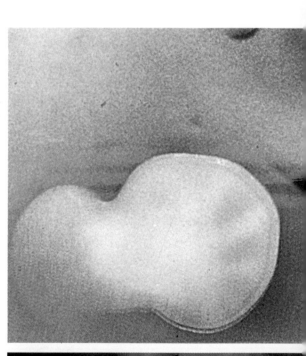

Close-up of the hand. The forearm is very short —what looks like a wrist is in fact the elbow. Along the contour of the hand, the skin has thickened to form a kind of ridge. The entire development of the arm is governed by inter-action between the cells in that ridge and the tissue inside.

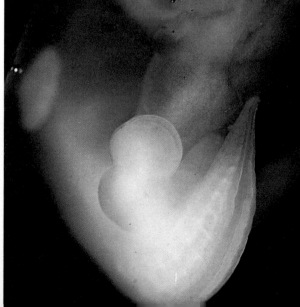

The foot and the leg assume their form the same way. Here, as well, the ridge is visible at the edge. The tail is falling more and more behind in its growth, and will soon end up com-pletely inside the body contours. It disappears almost entirely. Its substance is used in other regions.

Hand, foot, face

Hand, foot, and face are usually regarded as the most personal parts of a human being, those by which you recognize him or her. These sprouting hands and feet could actually belong to any human embryo. The face is expressionless, with large, wide-open eyes looking straight out to the sides like the eyes of a baby hare.

But there are still thirty-three weeks until the time of birth . . .

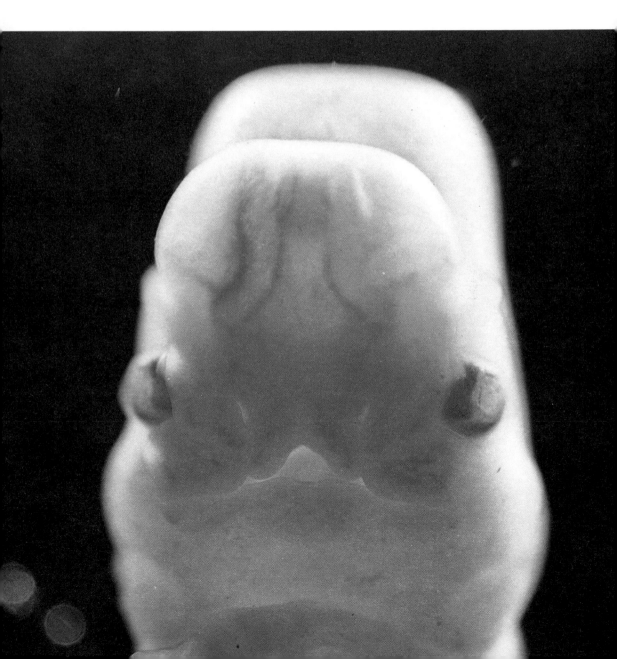

Design without a model

How can the cells of a developing embryo know what they are going to be? How can cells that have never seen a hand, let alone made one, know what to do? Nobody can give exact answers to these questions yet, but we are beginning to understand roughly what happens. The fact that the cells in the first cluster of cells begin to multiply at different paces, resulting in a rapidly growing vesicle and a more slowly developing "human seed," indicates that a certain fixed distribution of work can be arranged.

When the "human seed" has become a round disc with two layers, something very interesting occurs. A small group of cells on one edge takes command. They form a growth center. From this center a cord of cells begins to grow straight across the disc, between the two germ layers. The disc will thus have a longitudinal axis and the embryo a *notochord,* the predecessor of the backbone.

The notochord causes the "skin" covering it to thicken and form folds—the neural groove takes shape. Possibly the notochord also induces the middle layer to start its differentiation into segments. One step leads to the next.

Arm and leg buds form at both ends of a strip of condensed tissue along the sides of the trunk. Then the tissue in the buds swells out, causing the skin at the edge of the contour to thicken into a ridge. Keeping to a specific schedule, this ridge will influence the inner tissue to make fingers, hand, forearm, and upper arm, as well as the corresponding parts of the leg.

Should the ridge be interrupted in its work for some time, the part of the arm which was to be "ordered" then will be missing or poorly made. The ridge keeps to its schedule and cannot make up for what is lost. This is probably the case with many "building sites" in the body. There may be especially critical periods when they should not be disturbed.

We do not yet know how this "schedule" is carried out, what kind of chemical signals are emitted and received. It is amazing that the whole process works so elegantly in the overwhelming majority of cases.

The modeling of body and face, arms and legs involves a migration and flow of cells along certain definite tracks. It is believed that a kind of invisible pattern is created in the gelatinous mass, or *ground substance,* which fills out all the hollows of the primitive connective tissue in the middle layer of the embryo's body.

In the middle of the face, the forehead outgrowth known as a process—the origin of the nose and the middle part of the upper lip and upper jaw—will meet and join the two upper-jaw processes, which give rise to the cheeks and the remaining part of the upper jaw and upper lip. During the following weeks the nasal septum will descend and join the two halves of the palate, which turn up like gates from either side of the primitive mouth cavity and fuse in the middle. This makes a "two-story" arrangement: the mouth cavity with the palate as a ceiling, and a two-room second floor—the nostrils. The molecules in the ground substance direct the growth of these processes so that they will meet and fuse in the right place.

Along the sides of the trunk, cells which will give rise to the ribs are migrating in twelve streams. They meet in the front, in the center of the chest, where a breastbone begins to form. Between the ribs as well as in the body wall below the chest, future muscle cells are migrating. Right under the surface, the dermis begins to spread, beginning from the back and continuing out and around to the front. The cells of the thin outer layer begin to form the epidermis, where later on hair follicles, sebaceous (oil) glands, and sweat glands will be located.

Six weeks old

These two embryos are about the same age. The one to the right, however, is already one and a half times as long and seems far more developed. Individuals differ from the very beginning. Some of us are slow, others more precocious. The great differences in the beginning are due to the speed of growth. One millimeter (0.04 inch) a day is a lot for a creature tiny enough to stretch out on a thumbnail.

At 6 weeks, 1.5 cm (0.6 inch). The hands are developing fingers, but the arms are too short to meet. Between the hands we see the heart and the liver, separated by the diaphragm. The developing cerebral halves are shimmering through the skin of the forehead. ▶

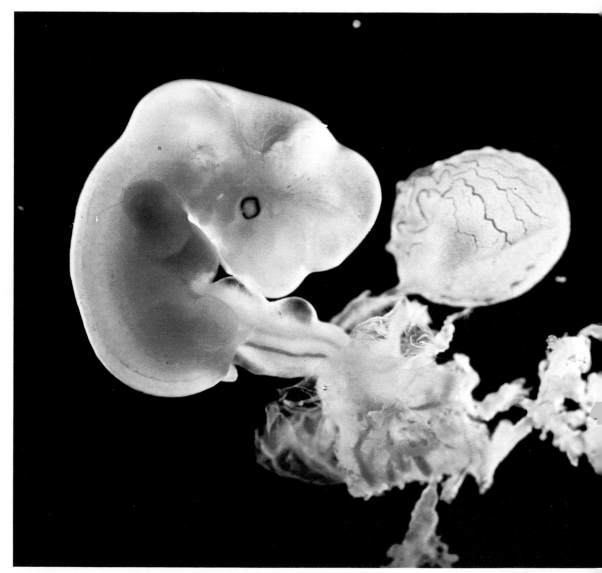

At 5½ weeks, 1 cm (0.4 inch). The head, the body, and the yolk sac are all about the same size. The yolk sac is still the main supplier of blood cells, since there is no bone marrow yet. The blood vessels in the yolk-sac wall are thick, as they are in the umbilical cord and the placenta. The major part of the blood circulation is outside the embryo.

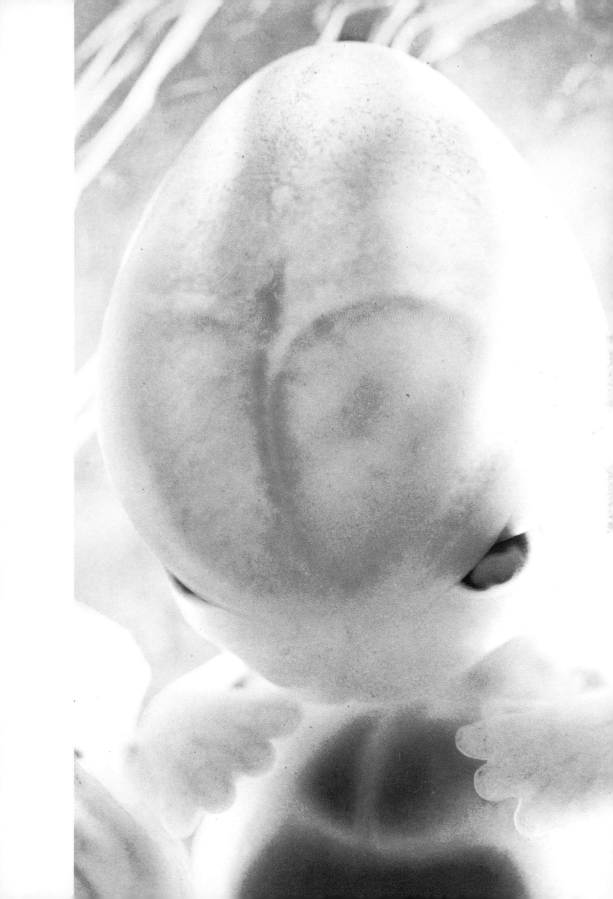

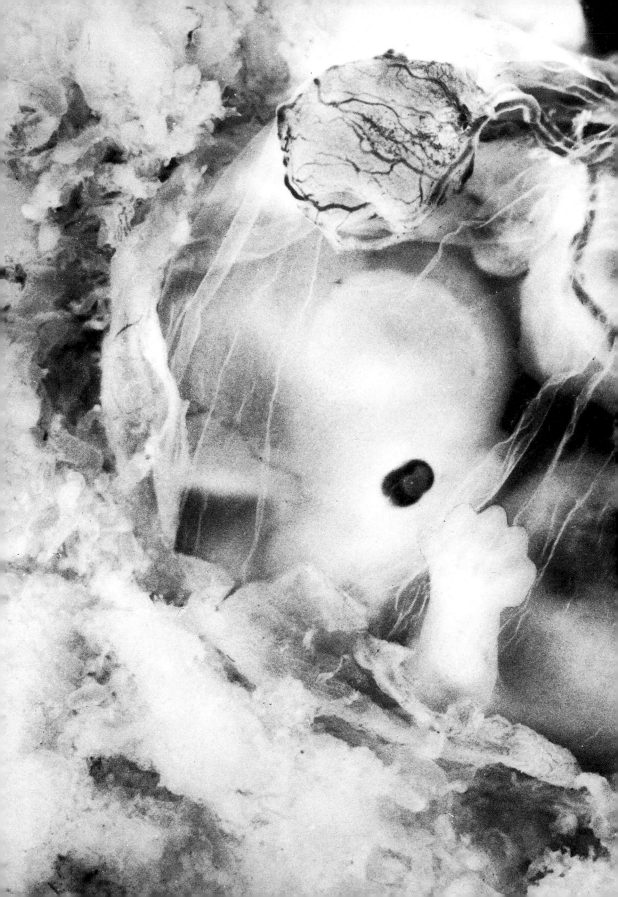

At 6 weeks, just under 1.5 cm (0.6 inch). The chorionic sac has been opened. The embryo rests on its placenta with the amnion (the inner fetal membrane) like an airy veil over it. The fingers are projecting, and the toes are not far behind. The yolk sac, on the other hand, has ceased to grow—the liver is now taking over the production of blood cells. The eye looks as if it will become double-barreled, but that is only a transitory stage.

At 6 weeks, 1.5 cm (0.6 inch). The chorionic sac has been completely removed. The embryo floats freely in the amnion, which is filled with fluid and still has ample space. The yolk-sac stem and the yolk sac itself are in the left corner.

The spine

Seen from behind, the six-week-old embryo looks relatively well proportioned. Somewhat chubby, perhaps, but most babies are.

But then we notice that the small tips below the shoulders are the future hands, and that a rather large tail is still curling between the legs. Moreover, what we see on top is not the head but the neck, since the head is still bent forward, with the chin on the chest. The head and neck are half the body length.

A newborn baby's head is a fourth of the body length. A four-year-old can try on Daddy's hat but not Daddy's suit. In an adult the head is one eighth of the body length. Obviously it is important that the head reach full development early.

At six weeks the embryo has only the beginnings of a skeleton. The spinal cord is shimmering through the thin skin. It is outlined by two delicately drawn red lines, the two vertebral arteries.

Around the spinal cord, development is in full swing. The somites join in the front of the cord to form the so-called *bodies of vertebrae* as well as the discs between them. On both sides of these bodies of vertebrae, outgrowths will form. These projections will gradually close like arches around the delicate nerve tissue of the spinal cord, and protect it.

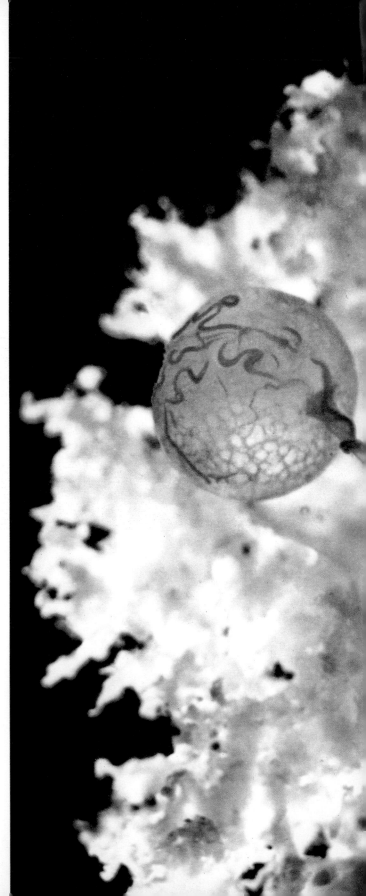

Six weeks since conception, four weeks since the menstrual period was skipped. In a few days the mother-to-be will know whether her next period will come or not.

Meanwhile, the embryo grows, secure in its cavity beneath the surface of the uterine lining. The placental cells still govern the production of hormones from the corpus luteum.

The embryo floats in its amniotic envelope. The dark area in the middle is the liver and the heart. To the left, the umbilical cord emerges with the yolk-sac stem. The cord leads to the placenta, behind the embryo and the yolk sac. Blood cells needed by the embryo are supplied through vessels which show clearly in the photo.

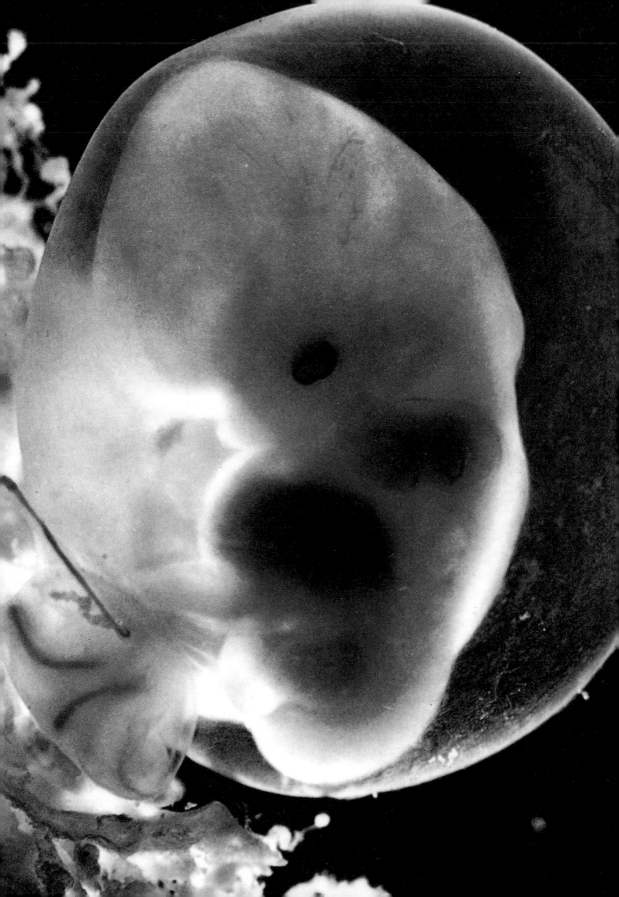

Is it healthy?

"Is it healthy?" This is the first question new parents ask as soon as they know whether their baby is a boy or a girl. They wonder if the baby has the right number of fingers and toes, whether everything is in place. Today's parents worry over the debate on drugs and environmental poisons, but the same question has always been asked by people who have just become parents. In the overwhelming majority of cases, the answer is yes.

But this fact is no consolation when something does go wrong. Statistics can tell only what has happened, not what is going to happen in the future.

Actually, it would be strange if nothing ever deviated from perfection, considering the millions of events which must follow in sequence during fetal development. For each fertilized ovum, it is, so to speak, the first attempt. Quite a number of such attempts end up as mere attempts. Some scientists calculate that, on an average, every second fertilization fails to produce a child.

Even when the ovular vesicle implants itself properly, menstruation is prevented, and the pregnancy test is positive, miscarriage occurs in about one case out of ten within the first three or four months. Among the embryos examined from such early miscarriages, up to 80 percent were so gravely malformed that they would not have been likely to survive after birth. In fetuses from late miscarriages as well, malformations are more common than in full-term babies. Nature obviously tries to sort out the ova, embryos, and fetuses which are not capable of surviving. In most cases it succeeds, and for this reason miscarriage should not always be regarded as a tragedy. Unfortunately, however, a small number of children are born deformed.

In the past when this happened it was believed that the

mother might have been frightened or injured (or possibly have committed a sin) during pregnancy. Today, environmental poisons and pharmaceutical preparations are the first things to be blamed. Actually, external factors seem to be responsible for only a small percentage of all malformations. Hereditary and other genetic factors account for a somewhat larger number. But for most malformations at birth, exact causes are yet to be found.

In regard to genetic hazards, it is possible today to consult specialists who will estimate the prospects for each couple. A number of conditions, including chromosomal abnormalities such as Down's syndrome, can be detected by taking samples from the amniotic fluid, making possible an abortion if the parents so desire.

X-ray examinations of a woman's lower abdomen are not made if it is possible that she is in early pregnancy. However, with today's methods, the dosage of radiation to which a fetus is exposed if a pelvic measurement is needed just before delivery is very low. The danger of radiation injury in the child is thousands of times less than the risk of injury during delivery should the pelvis be too narrow and no Caesarean section is performed. Efforts are now being made to replace X-ray with ultrasound, which is perfectly safe in the small quantities necessary. German measles during pregnancy used to be the cause of a number of fetal injuries; now there is an effective vaccine. The thalidomide tragedy has led to caution in the use of medication during early pregnancy. It should be emphasized, however, that old, well-known medicines have not become more dangerous; blind fear of drugs is not called for. The disease to be treated often might be a considerably greater threat to both mother and child than the drug prescribed for its treatment. And—as we said before—the overwhelming majority of children *are* healthy.

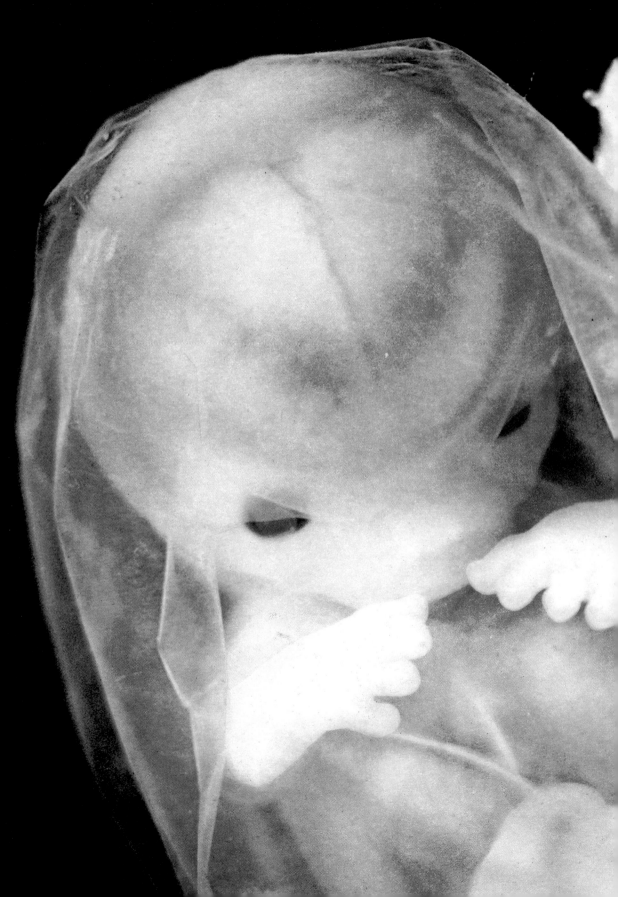

Farewell to the embryo stage

At eight weeks, 4 centimeters (1.6 inches), the developing individual is no longer an embryo, but a fetus. Everything that will be found in the fully developed human being has now been established. The fetal stage is a period of growth and perfection of detail. The heart has been beating for a month, and the muscles have just begun their first exercises. Two menstrual periods have now been skipped. At about this time the mother-to-be goes to a doctor or clinic for prenatal care.

Early pregnancy

When her menstrual period doesn't come as usual, every woman starts wondering. In many cases menstruation may be skipped for reasons other than pregnancy. The earliest time at which a pregnancy test can be done is about the tenth day after menstruation should have come.

Once she has learned that she is pregnant and has decided that she wants the child, a woman faces a great revolution in her life, which will never be the same. The changes begin rather slowly. Some women are nauseous or sick, but this usually passes. As time goes by, however, the woman will feel, with increasing intensity, an attachment to the new individual taking shape inside her. This can cause mixed feelings, mentally as well as physically. To have a child is something very common and very natural, but nevertheless it is a remarkable experience for the person involved.

To be pregnant also means that the woman must prepare herself to bear and take care of a child. There will be new demands and challenges, including some that parents might not think of, especially with the first child.

First visit

Depending upon the facilities in different parts of the country, a pregnant woman may receive prenatal care from a doctor, a midwife, or a specially trained nurse. To simplify this text, we generally refer to the "doctor" in discussing obstetric care.

At the first visit to the doctor or maternity clinic, a woman should bring evidence of health insurance and any record of her previous health. (In the United Kingdom a woman will normally be cared for during pregnancy and

childbirth under the National Health Service and at her first visit her medical history will be taken.) One of the first questions will be her age. A woman having her first baby is considered old at thirty-five; twenty to thirty is the best age. Of course, it is also important to know whether this is the first child.

Certain previous illnesses may require special care during pregnancy—for example, heart, liver, and kidney ailments. If they have been serious, pregnancy may involve danger for both child and mother. Tuberculosis and gonorrhea call for special vigilance. Diabetes requires additional attention, and usually special care; the insulin treatment must be carefully adjusted to the new strain put on the mother's system. It is also important to know about diabetes in other members of the family.

Miscarriage

Previous miscarriages, abortions, and the number of previous children are also recorded by the doctor or nurse. If a miscarriage has occurred in the second or third fetal month, it is often because something went wrong in the early formation of the fetus, as we said before. Frequent early miscarriage, however, requires further investigation; a battery of tests is available to determine the cause. For miscarriage which occurred later during pregnancy, a simple cause may sometimes be found. It may then be possible to intervene and correct the cause during the new pregnancy.

Examination

At the first examination, a urine sample is taken, to be tested for the presence of bacteria, sugar, and albumin. Two blood samples are taken. In certain states in the U.S., one sample is required by law for a syphilis test. This test is known as the Wassermann test, though methods other than those described by Wassermann are used today. Another blood sample is for determining blood group and the Rh type. Blood from a prick in the fingertip will show the hemoglobin content of the blood (hemoglobin is the substance giving the blood cells their color, and plays a vital

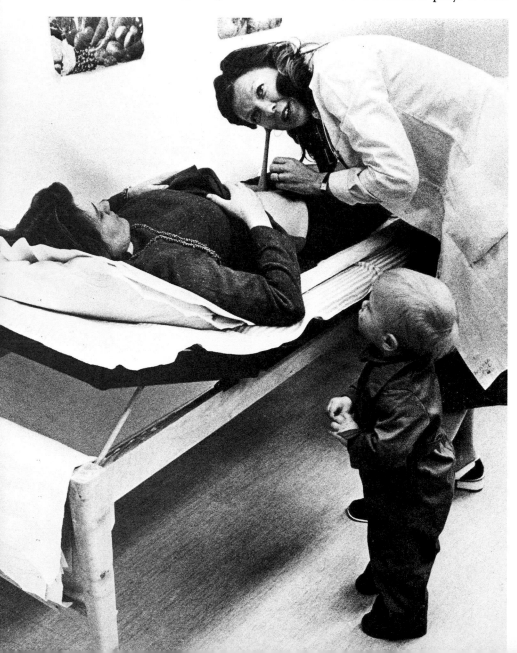

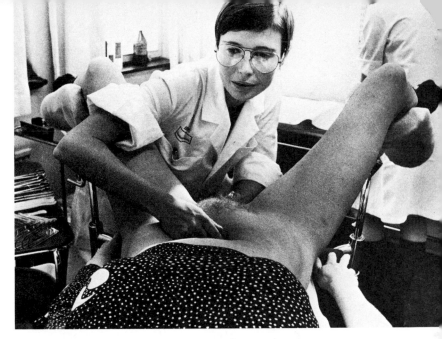

role in transporting oxygen in the body). A test for anti-bodies against rubella (German measles) and screening for antibodies against a panel of blood types are also frequently done.

After the samples are taken, an internal examination is performed. The doctor or nurse inserts a speculum into the vagina. The instrument permits inspection of the cervix, or mouth, of the uterus, which is bluish red and softened if a child is on the way. The doctor also feels the abdomen from outside while his or her fingers are inserted deeply into the vagina, to get an idea of the entire uterus, its size, form, and consistency. A Pap smear is generally done at this time, as well.

After the blood pressure is checked, the doctor listens to the heart. The breasts, too, are examined—are the nipples suitable for nursing? The usual check for lumps in the breast is also done.

When will the baby be born?

The average duration of a pregnancy is 280 days, calculated from the first day of the last menstrual period. Most babies—85–95 percent—are born between the 266th and the 294th days. Common deviations thus range up to 14 days in either direction. The usual way of calculating the child's birth date starts from the first day of the last period.

To this, 9 months and 7 days are added. This method of calculation is not quite accurate, because the ovum is usually released from the ovary 10–14 days after the first day of menstruation. Thus, during the first two weeks of the calculated time the woman is actually not pregnant at all. If the interval between the menstruations exceeds 28 days, ovulation is also likely to be late, delaying the fertilization of the ovum as well. If the duration of the menstrual cycle is not taken into account, the calculated birth date will be set too early.

If the mother has been using birth-control pills and then stopped because she wanted to have a child, it may be harder to predict when the child will be born. Several months may pass until ovulation occurs and menstruation returns. In addition to this, the interval between periods is often exceeded, since the ovular vesicle in the ovary needs more time to reach the stage of maturity when the ovum is released. A certain time may have to pass before the body has resumed its normal rhythm. If pregnancy occurs during this time, predicting a birth date becomes more difficult.

Advice for early pregnancy

In the beginning of pregnancy the woman feels as if the menstrual period may start at any moment. She experiences a feeling of heaviness in the lower abdomen because of the increased circulation of blood. The uterus is growing, and this may cause diffuse pain. The breasts increase in size, and the tenderness generally felt before menstruation does not go away.

All through the pregnancy, the woman is usually in touch with the doctor or clinic for monthly checkups. After the seventh month, she generally goes more often, sometimes once a week during the final month. She is given advice about maintaining her health and about danger signals to watch for.

Pregnancy affects the woman's whole system. At first she may tire easily and feel a great need to sleep. To a certain extent, she should give in to this need, which usually disappears later. Nausea and vomiting are not uncommon in the early months. Some women find that it helps to start the day with only a cup of tea and a cracker, and to stay in bed for a while. Several small meals are usually easier to keep down than a couple of large ones. If nausea causes too much trouble, the woman should speak to her doctor. All drugs and medicines should be taken with caution; medicines which a woman has taken all along might have a different effect now. Each should be discussed with a doctor. For women who take insulin or thyroid, the dosage must often be changed. However, as we said earlier, it is wrong to believe that all medicines are dangerous and should be avoided. Those drugs prescribed by a doctor should be taken. Iron, vitamins, and thyroid hormone, for example, may be vital to the fetus.

German measles is a disease requiring caution, because it is known to be the cause of severe malformations in the baby if the mother is infected in early pregnancy. If you have not been vaccinated or your immunity established by the test mentioned earlier, you should immediately notify your doctor or clinic if exposed. German measles is contagious only through direct contact with a sick person. Serological tests can determine whether infection has occurred. If so, the woman normally has the option of a therapeutic abortion.

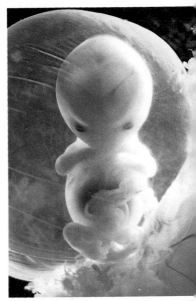

Seventh week,
2 cm (0.8 inch).

Food

A good diet during pregnancy is not very different from the well-balanced diet desirable at all times. The quality of the diet is more important than the quantity. A woman should gain roughly 20 percent of her initial weight during pregnancy, or about twenty-five pounds—a bit more for the tall and sturdy, somewhat less for short or small-boned women. Pregnancy is not a time for strict weight control. Obese women have a greater risk of complications in pregnancy and should consult with their doctors from the start.

The food should be rich in protein, to be found in meat, fish, eggs, dairy products, beans, and nuts. A variety of fruit and vegetables is also important. Whole-grain cereals and breads are to be preferred to pastries and cakes. Highly salted foods should also be avoided.

The fetus makes great demands—and these demands rank over those of the woman's own body. For example,

we know that approximately one third of the woman's iron reserve passes over to the fetus, to form its blood. There is not that much iron in the ordinary diet. Even if the woman is not anemic, she should still have an iron supplement. If a woman's diet does not seem to be well balanced, the doctor may prescribe other vitamin supplements. Folic acid is needed during pregnancy, and unless a woman's diet contains a large variety of leafy green vegetables and legumes, a supplement may be necessary. Dairy products (milk, cheese, yogurt, etc.) usually supply sufficient calcium. Additional doses of B vitamins and calcium are sometimes given for cramp in the calves.

The dentist

Pregnancy is no time to skip your usual visit to the dentist. Among other things, pregnancy causes changes in the gums, which should be watched. It is recommended that women visit the dentist at least once in early pregnancy, and once soon after delivery.

Tobacco and alcohol

Alcohol is perfectly safe in small quantities. Recent research suggests dangers to the fetus from heavy drinking. An occasional glass or two of wine, or a cocktail, will do no harm. Smoking should be avoided. It is not known whether smoking actually harms the fetus, but women who smoke often give birth to smaller babies. There is also evidence that babies whose mothers smoke have more respiratory diseases in early infancy.

Bathing and hygiene

Swimming, tub baths, and showers are as safe and healthy during pregnancy as at any other time. Since a pregnant woman has a greater tendency to get cramps, swimming alone should be done with caution.

Increased vaginal discharges are quite normal during pregnancy, so this area must be carefully washed. Curiously enough, there are women who have the idea that soap and water are harmful to one's genitals. On the contrary! Douching is not advisable during pregnancy (and is actually not necessary at other times, either). If the vaginal discharge seems to cause itching or soreness, this may indicate an infection, probably a fungus called *monilia*. This should be checked with the doctor, for treatment will make it disappear.

Breasts

The pregnant woman may want a well-fitting bra with broad shoulder straps to support and raise her breasts. They will soon get large and heavy, and the skin may stretch. The best way to treat sagging breasts is to see to it that they never develop. Examination of the breasts for lumps is as important now as at other times.

Sexual intercourse

A healthy mother-to-be can enjoy sex as often as she likes. During the nine months of pregnancy women may find that their desire for sex fluctuates. Since it is not necessary to worry about contraceptives, couples may feel a pleasant and unaccustomed freedom in their life together. Extra care for hygiene is appropriate, particularly close to the time for delivery, when the risk of infection may increase. Some doctors feel that for a woman with a tendency to miscarry it is wise to avoid intercourse in early pregnancy, although intercourse has never been proven to cause miscarriage.

Live as usual

This is good advice for pregnancy, along with avoiding all excesses. A woman should continue her employment as long as she wants to (and the company regulations permit her to). She should move around as usual and enjoy sports as usual, with the exception of sports involving violent physical contact. Special exercise during pregnancy to prepare for labor is discussed later. A regular program of exercise and fresh air is beneficial in every way, for body, child, and good spirits.

Third month

Two months and one week have passed since conception. The fetus is now well established. The placenta has taken over the production of all hormones necessary for the uterus to keep and nurture the developing child. The corpus luteum has done its part; from now on, the fetus will manage on its own. The actual size of the fetus can be seen in the drawing below.

In the third month the uterus fills up a large part of the pelvic cavity. The intestines are pressed upward, and the abdomen begins to get a little rounder.

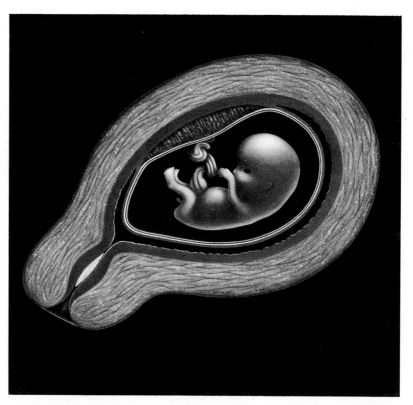

A placenta has grown around the spot where the tiny embryonic vesicle once landed. The fetus draws its nourishment through the umbilical cord. It floats in the fluid inside the amniotic sac (the inner fetal membrane), which, covered with the chorion (the outer fetal membrane), has grown so that it now fills most of the uterus. In the large photo to the right, the chorion has been opened and pulled aside.

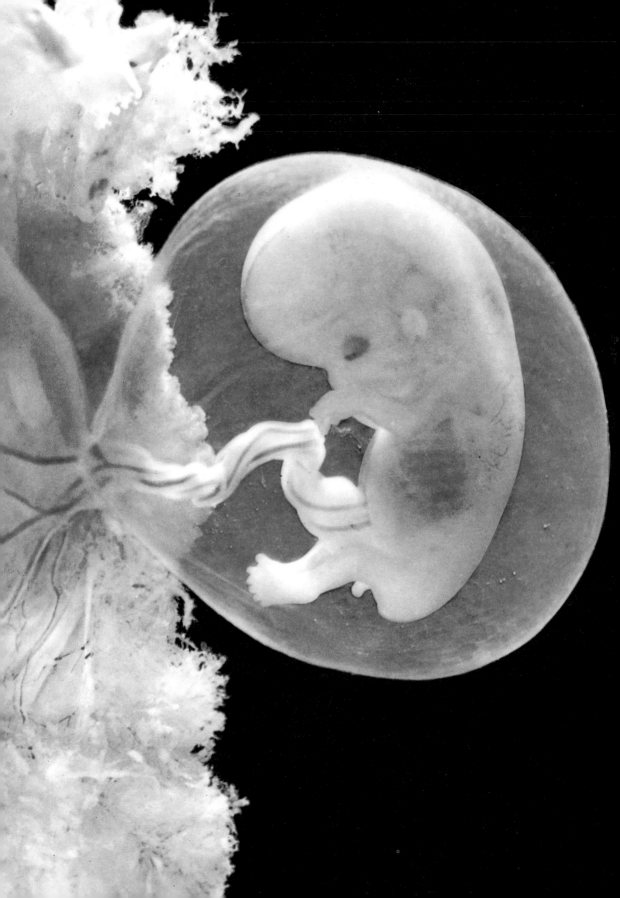

Boy or girl?

The child's sex is determined at the moment of conception. If a Y sperm is the first to reach the ovum (which always has an X chromosome), the new individual will have the combination XY in its twenty-third pair of chromosomes and become a boy. With an X sperm instead, the combination XX arises, and the child will be a girl. It is possible to examine the chromosomes of the fetal cells floating freely in the fetal waters, and thus find out the sex of the fetus. However, usually such an examination is made only in the course of testing for suspected hereditary disease or chromosomal abnormality. To most parents, the child's sex is a well-kept secret up to birth.

During the first quarter of the development, the sexes are exactly alike, with the same primordial sex glands and organs. The further development of these glands and organs is then determined by the sex chromosomes.

At 9 weeks, 4–5 cm
(just under 2 inches) ▶

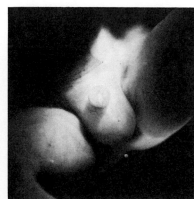

This fetus is a boy. In both sexes development starts with a bud at the top of a slit and a swelling on either side. Here the bud will develop into a penis, and the swellings fuse together to form a pouch: the scrotum, into which the testicles will descend.

At 15 weeks, 14 cm (5.6 inches)
At 16 weeks, 16 cm (6.4 inches)

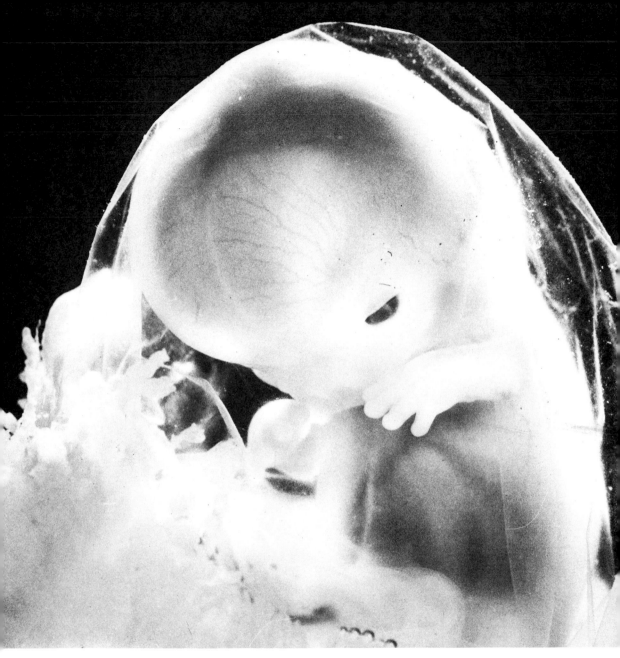

This fetus is a girl. Her external genitals do not depart so far from the primary stage. The bud becomes the clitoris, and the swellings turn into the labia. The slit between them does not close. Both the urethra and the vagina will open into it.

At 11–12 weeks,
10 cm (about 4 inches)
At 19 weeks, 20 cm (8 inches)

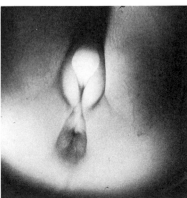

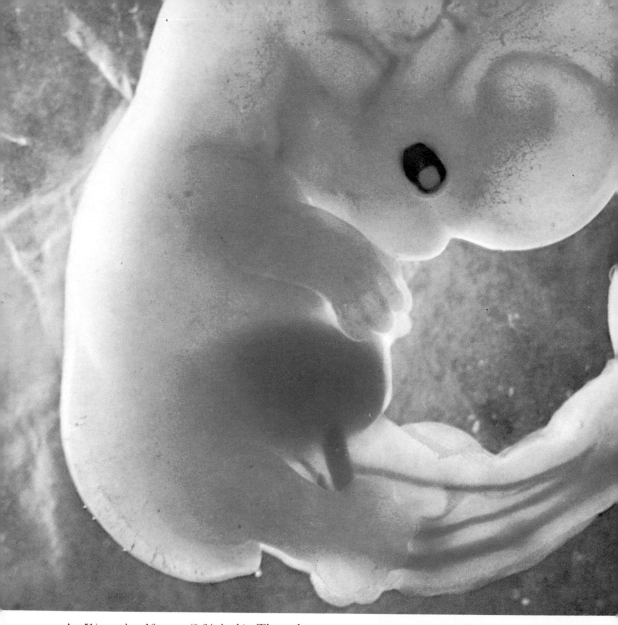

At 5½ weeks, 16 mm (0.64 inch). Through the large umbilical vein, the thickest vessel, blood returns from the placenta with oxygen and nourishment. Before it is readmitted into the fetal circulatory system, this blood is shunted straight through the as-yet-immature liver, the large red shadow under the hand. The woman's liver still does all the work.

About 5 weeks, 1.5 cm (0.6 inch). The yolk sac is still producing blood cells, but the liver is gradually taking over. The heart has begun its differentiation into the atria and the ventricles, but the partitions and valves are not yet present.

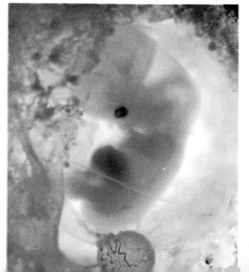

Blood circulation

Without blood circulation we would not be able to live and grow. As the system of the fetus gets larger, there are increased demands for rapid transport of oxygen, nourishment, and waste products. In the beginning the vessel system is made up of a number of simple tubes, through which flows a rich fluid. Dissolved in this fluid, oxygen and other substances are transported. But soon increasingly specialized cells will appear in the fluid: the red blood cells, highly effective transporters of oxygen, and the white blood cells, constituting the body's defense against foreign intruders, bearing the instructions as to what belongs in the body and what is foreign and must be expelled.

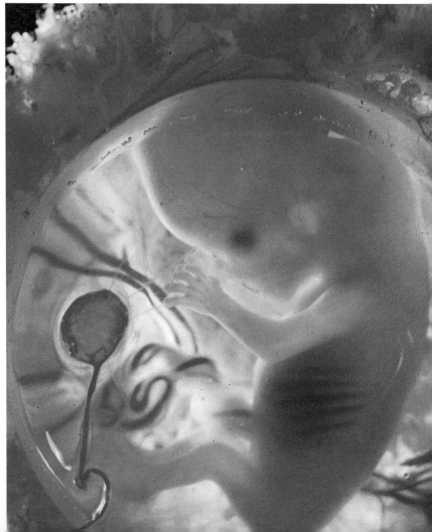

At 11 weeks, 6 cm (2.4 inches). The yolk sac is no longer active; its stem will soon loosen from its attachment. Blood cells are now produced by the liver and the spleen, and soon the bone marrow will take over. Lymphocytes, the white blood cells concerned with immunity, are now being formed in the lymph nodes and thymus. The heart is complete.

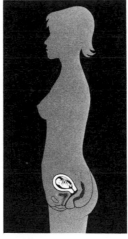

During the fourth month of pregnancy, the fetus will grow from 5 cm (2 inches) to more than 10 cm in length. The top of the uterus now reaches to halfway between the pubic bone and the navel. Clothes must be let out at the waist.

Fourth month

Eleven weeks have passed since conception, thirteen since the last menstruation began. The mother-to-be enters her fourth month.

The fetus is already assuming "full-term" proportions. The head is now about one third of the body length with legs outstretched. The ribs are clearly visible, and the first cores of bone tissue appear in the cartilaginous pre-stages of the skeleton. Here the chorion is again folded back, and we look through the thin amniotic membrane. Like a wreath encircling it lies the rich network of placental root threads.

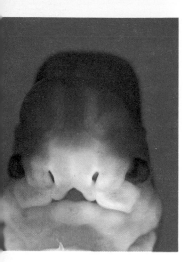

The face

Creating a face is actually quite a complicated affair. The process might be described as five peninsulas growing forth and joining underneath the skin. The first peninsula proceeds down between the eyes. It ends in a "bay" on each side—the future nostrils—and thus forms the nose and the middle of the upper lip. Then two other peninsulas appear under the eyes and form the cheeks and the sides of the upper lip. Finally, under the mouth, the last two peninsulas will meet and fuse in the middle to form the lower lip and the chin.

Eventually, the facial muscles will shape the nostrils, the lips ("Cupid's bow"), and all the other features which lend character to a face.

At 5 weeks, 6 mm (0.24 inch). The "bays" are still open—the gap between the nostrils and the edge of the upper lip is not yet obliterated. A small nick will remain where the sides fuse to the central part.

At 8–9 weeks, 3 cm (1.2 inches). The "seams" do not show any more. Eyelids have begun to form. The nose is short and snub, and the ear starts to take shape. The face begins to look human, seven and a half months before birth.

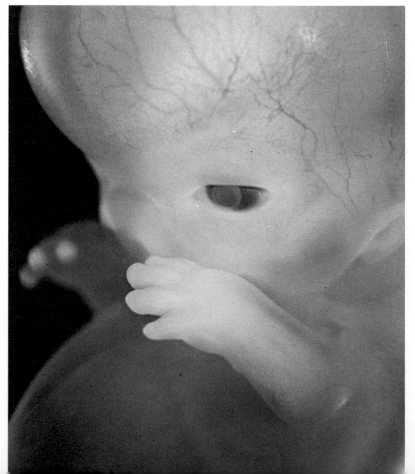

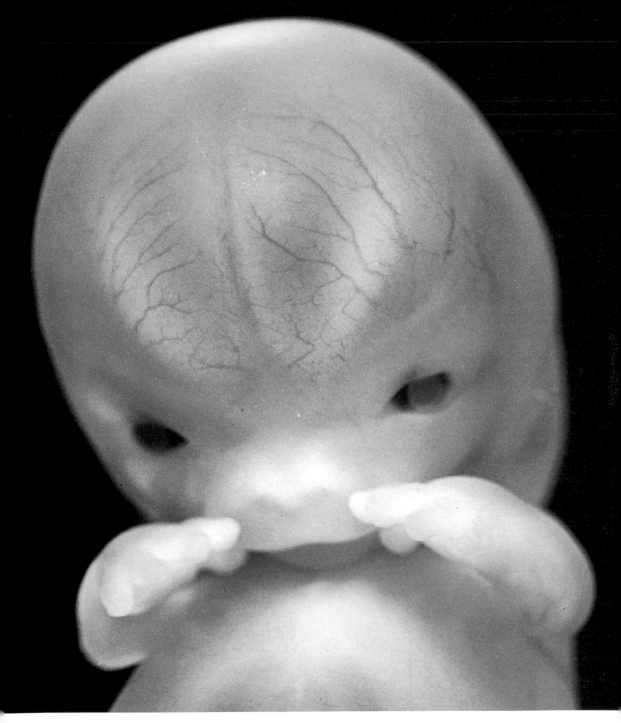

At 5–6 weeks, about 1.5 cm (0.6 inch)

Profile at eleven weeks

At eleven weeks old, 5 centimeters (2 inches) long, the eyes are closed; the black pigment of the retina is shimmering through the delicate skin. The face has already assumed a baby's profile, with a large, rounded forehead, a tiny snub nose, and a definite chin. Muscles are already at work under the skin, and their movements become gradually more coordinated by the developing nervous system. The lips open and close, the forehead wrinkles, the brows —that is, the area of skin where they will be located—rise, and the head turns. All these motions will gradually develop into searching and sucking reflexes, vital when the newborn baby is to find the breast and start eating. The facial expression will also signal to adults how the baby feels and if it wants something. Wordless language is necessary at first. This is no heavyweight exercising his muscles —the fetus weighs three quarters of an ounce, the weight of an ordinary letter.

Arms and legs are now in constant motion, though their waving and kicks are too weak to be felt by the woman.

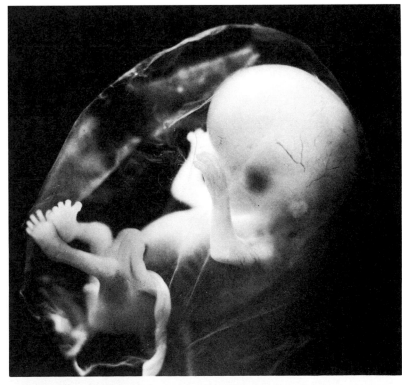

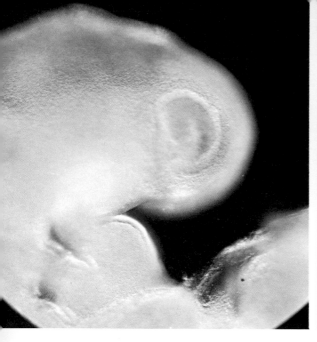 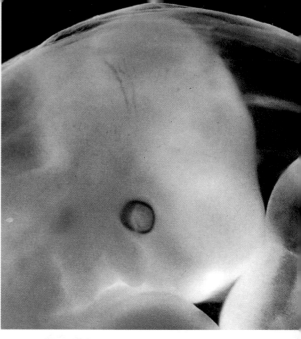

At 4 weeks, 4 mm (0.16 inch). The brim of the eye cup is shimmering through. The faint oval in the middle is the thin bubble pinched off by the skin to form a lens.

At 5 weeks, 7–8 mm (just under 0.33 inch). The eye shows as a black ring—dark pigment has formed in the wall of the cup, the future retina.

Eyes

The creation of an eye is a remarkable example of the interaction—one could almost say the dialogue—between the developing brain and the thin skin of the embryo.

First, the anterior part of the brain sends out a hollow stem to each side. The end of the stem expands to form a vesicle. When the vesicle approaches the surface of the skin, it turns inward like a cup—fundus and retina are established. At the same time, instructions are forwarded to the skin, "Make a lens!" The skin then pinches off a bubble, which is placed in the opening of the cup, forming a lens. Then, "Make a cornea!" And the skin covering the lens transforms itself into a thin, transparent cornea. On the front of the lens, the iris grows from the edges inward. Finally the surrounding skin is folded and forms two eyelids. The eye is complete.

The eyes of the newborn (*right*)—do they see? Yes, they receive visual sensations, and can follow certain objects dangled before them. Recent research indicates that they will even alert to a pattern resembling a face. But a long time will pass until the brain learns how to interpret visual images and understand the message from the eye.

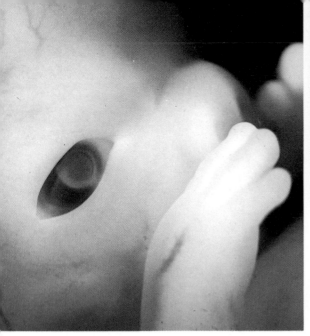

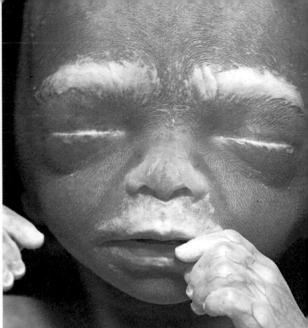

At 8 weeks, 3 cm (1.2 inches). Indications of eyelids. The pigment is still shimmering through the developing white. In the center of the pale iris you can see the pupil. At this stage it is covered by a thin membrane.

At 20 weeks, 21 cm (8.4 inches). The eyes are closed, like the eyes of a newborn kitten. The eyelids grow together in the beginning of the third month, and open again during the seventh.

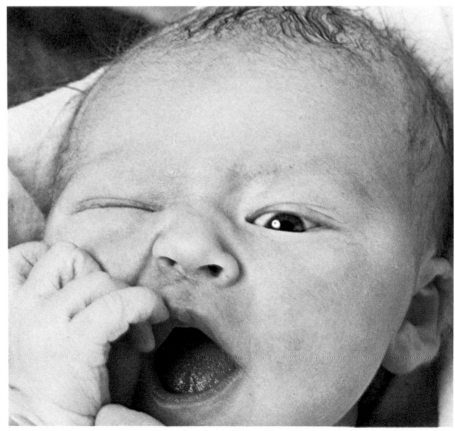

It is not especially remarkable that the newborn baby knows how to kick and grasp. Hands and feet have been practicing long before the day of delivery. The woman surely knows that the fetus can kick.

Hand and foot

In the fourth week after conception a stripe will appear along both sides of the trunk. This stripe is a thickening of the connective tissue of the middle germ layer, which is the origin of the muscles and the skeleton. Most of the stripe will become the thoracic and abdominal muscles, but at each end more will happen: An arm and a leg will be formed. As early as the fifth week, arm and leg buds protrude, covered by the thin embryonic skin. The buds are somewhat flat; they have an edge. Chemical signals are then emitted from the connective tissue, causing the edge to thicken into a ridge. This ridge reacts in turn by sending instructions to the connective tissue to make preparations for upper arm and thigh, forearm and lower leg, hand and foot, all in the proper order. Everything proceeds according to a specific schedule in a constant interaction between the connective tissue and the ridge, just as the brain and the embryonic skin work together to make the eyes.

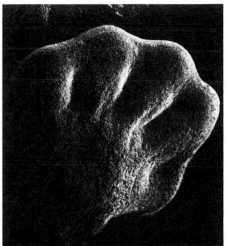

At 6 weeks, 12–13 mm (about 0.5 inch). *Left:* The foot with its ridge, where indications of toes will begin to show. The tail can be seen as a small tip now regressing. *Right:* the hand is a bit ahead in its development, with clear indications of fingers.

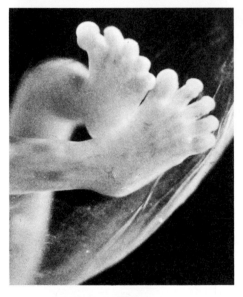

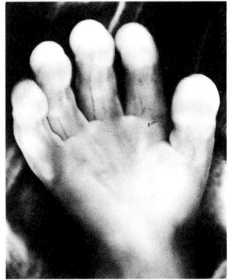

At 11 weeks, 5 cm (2 inches). The nail beds on toes and fingers are established. The muscles are exercising energetically.

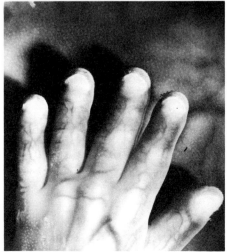

At 5 months, 25 cm (10 inches). The hands and the feet have been complete for some time. Sometimes the thumb slips into the mouth.

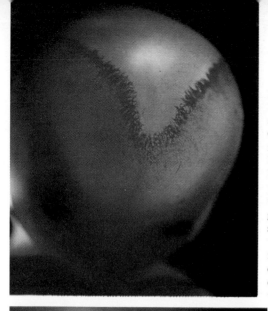

By the end of the seventh week a broad front of blood vessels can be seen advancing toward the crown. Cerebral membranes form, with a fluid between them so that the brain rests in a shock-absorbing bath. Primordial bone tissue is prepared at the base of the skull. From these primordia, the skull bones grow out like thin plates under the skin, up toward the crown. At the time of the delivery the skull bones must still be able to glide alongside each other; the top of the skull does not close until the baby is a year and a half old.

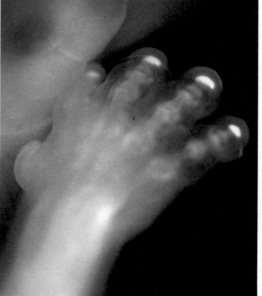

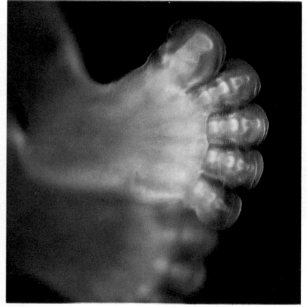

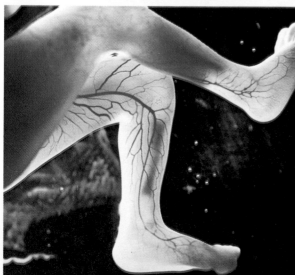

The two pictures above show hands and feet after approximately 8 weeks. The cartilaginous models of finger and toe joints show distinctly.

Left: At 4 months, 16 cm (6.4 inches). The bone core filling the cartilaginous model can be seen in the middle of the lower legs. These bone cores grow out toward both ends to replace the gristle, but the gristle grows too. That's the way we grow—gristle grows first, then the bone gradually replaces the gristle. Around the age of twenty-five the development of bones is finished.

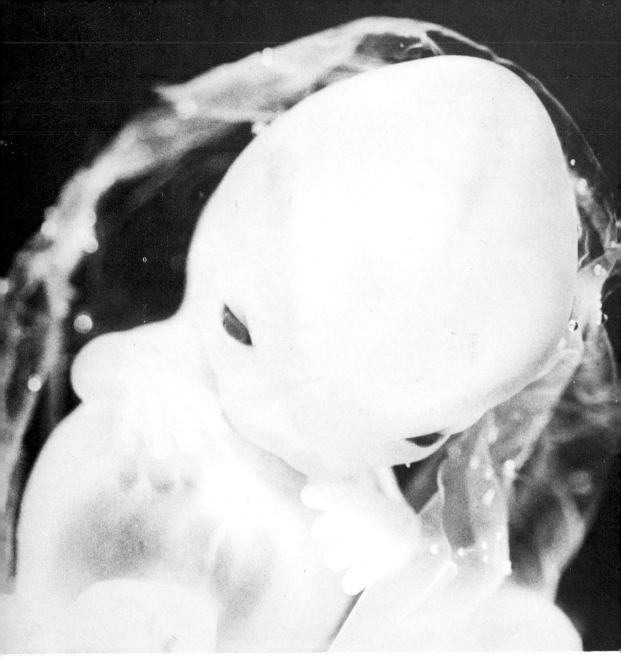

At 8 weeks, about 2.5 cm (1 inch). The cartilaginous precursors of the skeleton have been established.

Bones

The skeletal bones form two ways: either directly, which is the case especially with the skull bones, or by successively replacing a cartilaginous model with bone tissue. The skeleton is not fully developed until the age of twenty-five; fractures in young children heal wondrously well, without leaving the slightest trace.

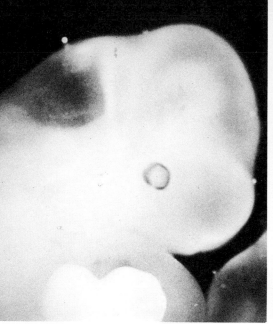

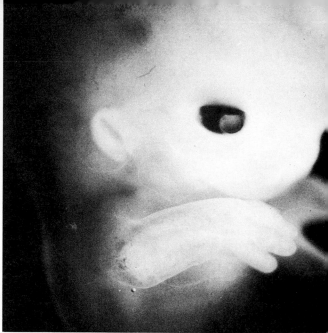

At 5 weeks, about 1 cm (0.4 inch). The developing outer ear looks like a somewhat wrinkled mouth just above the shoulder. Farther up you can catch a glimpse of a pale, oval contour between the outer ear and the depression of the rear brain curve—that is the bubble that was pinched off to become the inner ear.

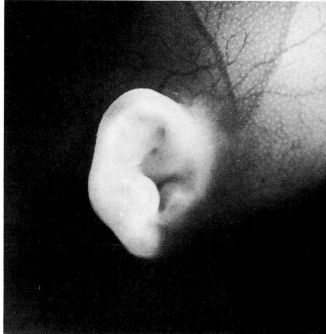

In the two pictures above and the large picture to the right, we see the outer ear taking shape, from simple skin folds at eight weeks, the "cauliflower ear" at four months, and the practically complete ear just over a month later. The shell-like part of the ear is known as the *concha*. The edge will start to roll in, and the small nick on top that most of us have means that the rolling was not quite perfect.

Ears

The ear consists of three different parts, and originates in three different regions. In the fourth week a bubble is turned inward from the skin on both sides of the rear part of the brain. This bubble will later become the inner ear, with its auditory and balance organs. In the fifth week the outer ear, with the auditory canal and the outer side of the eardrum, is developed at the upper end of the first gill groove (the rest will close). From the pharynx, a bulge of mucous membrane emerges, giving rise to the middle ear, where primordia of the auditory bones develop into malleus, incus, and stapes (the hammer, anvil, and stirrup). The middle ear will maintain its connection with the air passages through the Eustachian tube.

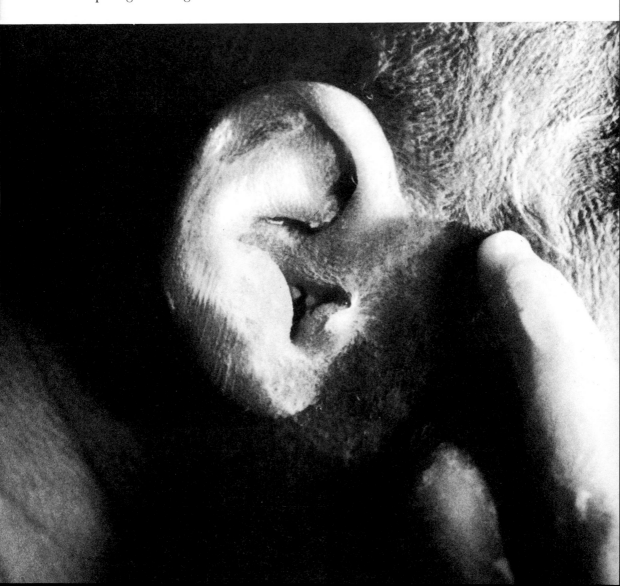

Halfway to birth

In the middle of the fifth month, half the pregnancy has passed. The fetus is already 15 centimeters (6 inches) long. By the end of the month it will be 25 centimeters (10 inches)—about half of the length of the newborn baby. This is quite an impressive pace, considering that it all started from an ovum just over a tenth of a millimeter (0.005 inch) in diameter. This growth rate will gradually slow down—a two-year-old has already reached half its adult body length.

There is room to move around now. Between the sixteenth and the twentieth weeks the woman feels the first faint kicks . . .

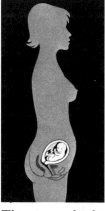

The top of the uterus will soon reach the level of the navel. The abdomen is getting rounder. The breasts, too, grow as a preparation for breast-feeding. Stirring motions, like little twitches, can be felt through the expanded uterine wall, but it is not yet possible to distinguish the different parts of the fetus.

Later pregnancy

The early fetal motions feel like the flutter of a fish tail, says Sigrid Undset in her novel, *Kristin Lavransdatter*. At first it is like a sort of bubbling in the lower abdomen, easily confused with intestinal rumblings. A woman carrying her first child will generally feel the stirring around the twentieth week; women who have had children before feel them somewhat earlier. The fetus, however, has been moving long before the woman noticed anything. It moves as soon as arms and legs begin to form. In the past, the time when the woman first felt the child-to-be move was known as the "quickening."

Nausea will usually have ceased when the woman has reached the tenth week. Feelings of depression, which may occur in the beginning, will also usually be gone at this time. The woman feels well and is filled with confidence.

Clothing

In the expressions of those meeting her, the woman can see that they notice she is pregnant. She has been forced to let out her skirt or pants at the waist, and loose, flowing tops are more comfortable. Light clothes are usually better; a woman often feels hot during pregnancy. Few women use maternity girdles any more. Today's women do not try to dress in a way that "it does not show." They are proud of the state of affairs, and have nothing to conceal, which gives them freedom to dress the way they like. Women with low arches may feel the need for arch supports as the body gets heavier. Shoes with high heels are awkward and may cause back strain. Tight shoes may seem tighter, because of fluid retention.

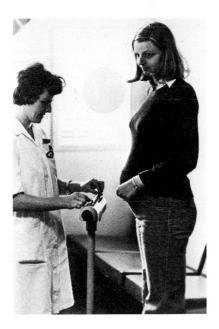

Medical checkups

The medical checkups at this time are often quite short. Blood and urine samples are taken regularly; weight is checked, and the woman has an opportunity to ask questions.

The doctor checks that the cervical canal is properly closed. In some cases it may prove too weak to withstand the increasing pressure exerted by the fetus. The canal may then dilate too early. This can be prevented by constructing a "cerclage": The cervical passage is held closed with an encircling suture. The doctor also checks that the uterus has grown properly. It should, as we said, have reached approximately the level of the navel. The fetal heartbeat can now be heard with a stethoscope.

Twins?

Most mothers wonder about the possibility of twins, which occur about once every ninety births. If the uterus is larger than expected, especially if it has expanded sideways more than usual, the doctor will suspect twins. Confirmation of this comes when the doctor can hear two fetal heartbeats. Although new electronic devices make the detection of multiple births much easier, there are still twins who arrive as a surprise.

Narrow pelvis

This is an uncommon complication. With today's ultrasound and X-ray techniques, it is easy to measure whether the pelvis is large enough. Moreover, thanks to rising standards of living (involving, among other things, a good diet), a narrow pelvis has become unusual in the developed nations. Formerly a great threat to both mother and child, a narrow pelvis is not so serious nowadays. If necessary, the child can be delivered by Caesarean section, through an incision in the abdominal wall. This operation only slightly increases the risk to the mother, as compared to an ordinary delivery. The operation may or may not be repeated for subsequent deliveries.

Varicose veins

These are a rather common complication of pregnancy. If they do not recede by themselves after childbirth, the doctor may recommend treatment. During pregnancy the woman should use elastic stockings as soon as varicose veins begin to show. Such stockings keep the veins from enlarging and improve the circulation of blood; so-called support stockings are not effective enough. The elastic stockings should be put on before getting up in the morning: The legs are first massaged in an upward direction toward the groin until all swelling disappears; then the stocking is turned inside out except for the foot portion and rolled on. Resting with the legs elevated also helps.

Hemorrhoids

These are actually varicose veins in the rectal opening. The growing uterus increases the pressure in the veins, causing them to dilate. The straining over a bowel movement which accompanies constipation may aggravate this condition. A high-bulk diet, plenty of fluids, exercise, and regular visits to the toilet will help prevent the formation and the discomfort of hemorrhoids. A warm bath is often

Both health and patience usually benefit when
a woman keeps on working.

Continuing to work can mean a variety of jobs, but more often than not it also means keeping a household going. The children who are already born need just as much attention as ever.

soothing. The doctor may also prescribe a cooling anesthetic salve or rectal suppositories.

Leg cramps, heartburn, and constipation

Leg cramps can be a problem in pregnancy. We mentioned earlier that large amounts of vitamin B may help to prevent them. Leg cramps can often be stopped by walking about, or with heat and massage. Heartburn is another common problem. It can be alleviated by eating smaller, more frequent meals, or with antacid preparations, preferably recommended by a doctor. Ordinary baking soda should not be used, however, since its sodium content might promote swelling.

If constipation occurs, it can be remedied by an improved diet. Whole-grain bread and cereals, fruit, vegetables, and other high-bulk foods are recommended. Large amounts of water are important, especially in the morning. Exercise also helps. Laxatives should be avoided unless recommended by the doctor.

The nipples

These should receive special care starting about the middle of pregnancy. The breasts produce a fluid which oozes out, and as it dries it hardens into something almost similar to scabs. The nipples should be washed carefully with luke-warm water and soap, and an ointment containing lanolin or another lubricant applied to keep them flexible. This will prepare them for nursing and avoid chapped or tender nipples. Inverted nipples can often be brought out with massage.

Toxemia

This is a disease which occurs only during pregnancy. It has several symptoms: Hands, feet, and face swell, weight increases, albumin appears in the urine, and blood pressure rises. These are warning signals. If they are not heeded, convulsions may occur. The toxemia has then become the very serious condition known as *eclampsia*. Vigilant prenatal health care can prevent this complication or at least make it less serious. A well-balanced diet also reduces the incidence of toxemia. Rest, possibly sick leave from work, and restricting salt are helpful. If the symptoms continue, the woman is usually put into the hospital for further treatment and, if necessary, early delivery of the baby.

Infections

Unnecessary exposure to any virus diseases, including colds, should be avoided. Even a harmless infection may involve risks at the time of delivery. Exposure to any contagious diseases, such as hepatitis, venereal diseases, or German measles, should obviously be reported to the doctor. Fever blisters (herpes) should also be reported.

It is important to keep on with prenatal exercises. Arching and swaying, as the women on the following page are doing, strengthens and relaxes the back. Pregnant women usually enjoy meeting one another in these classes and comparing notes. The gymnastics may be performed in many ways. The instructor explains the principle of the exercises, which can then be done at home.

Prenatal exercise and childbirth education

The woman will feel better, and her abdominal muscles and her back will become stronger, if she takes part in gymnastic exercises during pregnancy. A further advantage

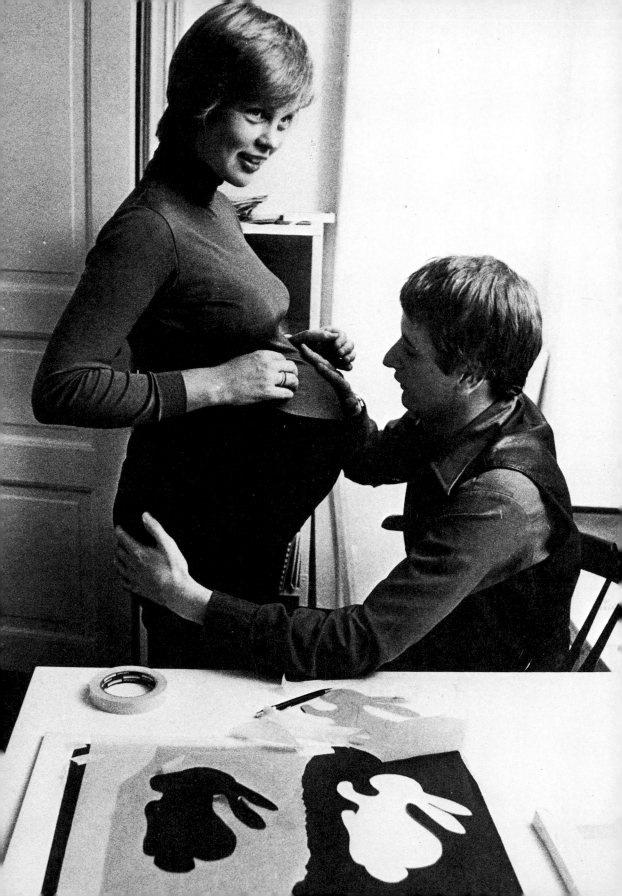

When you get bigger, a friendly tap on your stomach may be very reassuring. Many women keep working until the last moment; they will be away from work for some time afterward.

of a prenatal exercise program can be an easier delivery. If your doctor or hospital cannot direct you to childbirth classes in your community, write the International Childbirth Education Association, P.O. Box 20852, Milwaukee, Wisconsin 53220, for addresses of local groups. In England, the National Childbirth Trust, 4 Queensborough Terrace, London W2 3TB, may be of help.

No one should expect that the gymnastics and relaxation exercises will automatically ensure a painless delivery. But they are one of the things a woman can do to help her take a more active part in delivery. Moreover, she will feel much better during her pregnancy. The advantages to the newborn baby of less or no anesthesia have also been emphasized by recent research.

The discomfort and back strain caused by the ever-increasing dimensions of the abdomen can be avoided with the proper exercises. The muscles of the back are exposed to greater strain because of the increasing weight in the front. This strain may cause unnecessary tensions, which can be counteracted by some basic back-strengthening exercises. These should, of course, be followed at home as well as in the classes. Women with a previous history of backache or spinal disorder should consult their doctor or an orthopedist before engaging in these exercises.

The muscles of the pelvic floor are also trained in prenatal exercises. One of these consists in squeezing as though trying to keep from urinating. With the large muscles pressing the buttocks together, the woman should tighten the sphincter muscles in the pelvic floor. This exercise can be practiced at home by squeezing two fingers put into the vagina. Once it is clear how this movement feels, squeezing can be done without inserting the fingers. This exercise should be done several times daily. It helps prevent any slackening of the muscles after childbirth. Such slackening can make it hard to control urination. Coughing, sneezing, or straining can cause a small leak of urine. A new mother should continue this exercise, and

Some childbirth classes make it possible for prospective mothers and fathers to visit a delivery room and become familiar with its equipment. They can look at the delivery bed and learn how anesthesia is given and everything else that happens during a delivery. Breathing exercises are one of the most important parts of the psychoprophylactic training. On the top of the following page we see the instructor using a stopwatch to check that the mother-to-be has learned the correct rhythm. The father-to-be is generally just as interested and absorbed by what is going to happen. He can be of great assistance to the woman when she is practicing her breathing control.

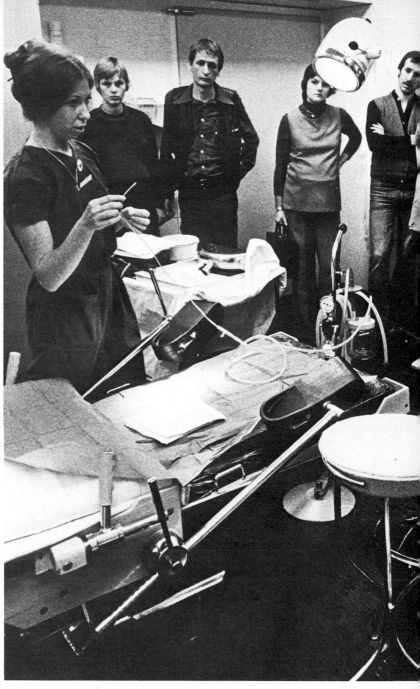

others learned in her classes, as soon as she has recovered from the delivery.

There are several methods now in use to facilitate the delivery both physically and mentally. These methods, called *psychoprophylactic* (from *psyche*: mind or soul, and

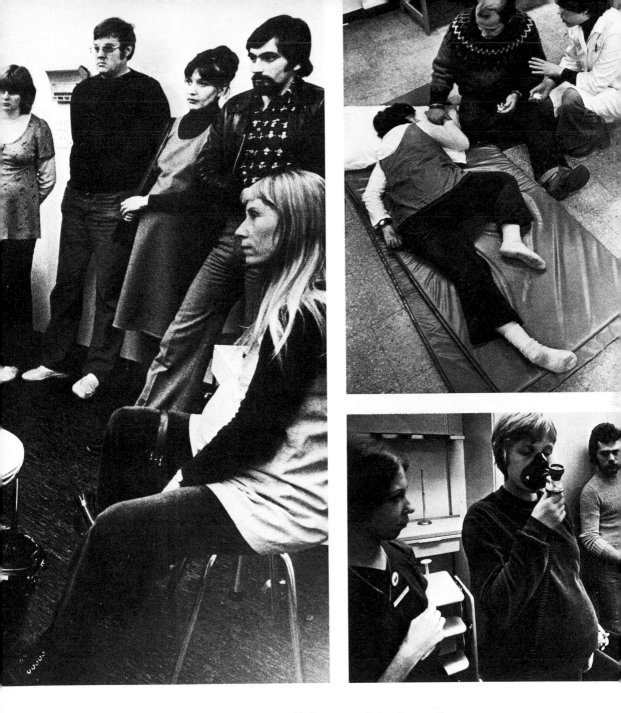

prophylaxis: prevention), can all be traced back to the discovery of the conditioned reflex made by the Russian physiologist Pavlov. Thanks to this, a person can be trained to respond with the correct action in a given situation without actually thinking. Through training it is thus possible to condition the woman to relax and concentrate on stimuli other than the pain of uterine contractions. This training can be combined with the prenatal exercises.

One of the earliest of such methods is the Lamaze system, started by Dr. Fernand Lamaze, who, along with Dr. Grantly Dick-Read, was a pioneer of so-called natural childbirth. By means of active breathing exercises following a carefully elaborated schedule, women following this method learn to stay calm and to control the pace of the final stages of delivery. In a great number of cases these various methods have enabled the mother to undergo the whole delivery without anesthesia—an experience considered by many women one of the peak moments in their

The childbirth training follows the actual course of childbirth as much as possible. As a result, women do not feel at the mercy of something unfamiliar, of strange hospital machinery. These pictures show a rehearsal and the actual event side by side.

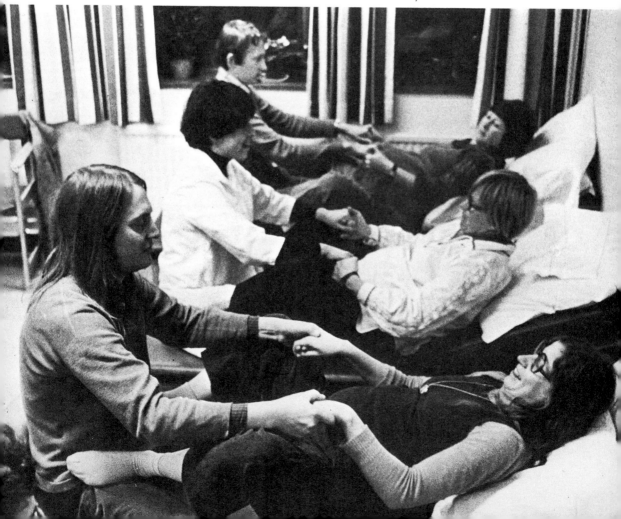

lives. All these methods can be combined with other forms of pain relief: analgesics, local anesthetics, epidural or spinal anesthetics. The fact that these drugs are available is a great source of comfort to childbearing women today.

Another reason for the effort to minimize the use of drugs is their effect on the newborn. Babies whose mothers have received little or no medication are generally more alert and responsive in the first hours and days of their lives. This, in turn, has an effect on the early mother-infant relationship.

In childbirth classes both parents also learn in detail what happens during delivery. This knowledge removes many misapprehensions, and the whole process becomes more natural and familiar.

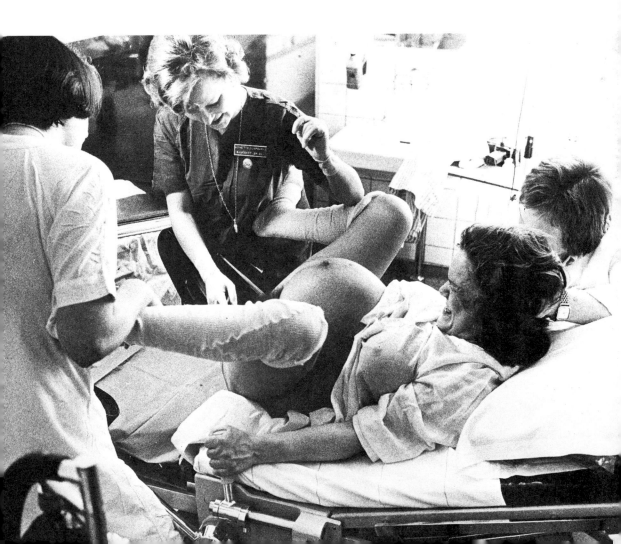

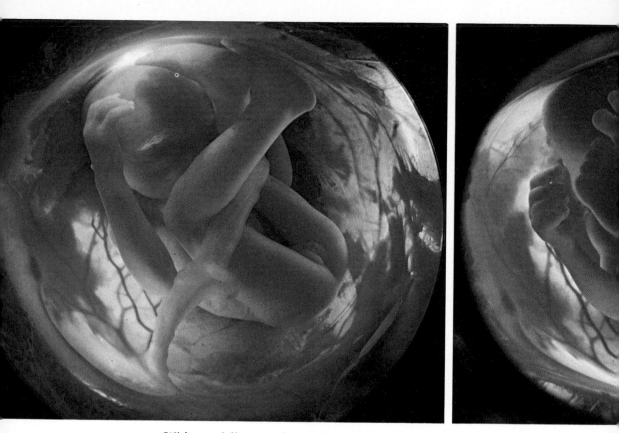

With specially manufactured equipment—a super-wide-angle lens with an ultrashort focal length—the whole fetus is photographed

What can the fetus hear?

The ears of the fetus function as early as the fourth month, and there is evidence that it hears a good deal. One might object that if a person dives under water and someone else talks to him, he hears only a muffled sound. This is true. The sound is muffled by the cushion of air remaining in the auditory canal outside the eardrum. But the fetus living in the amniotic fluid has no muffling air cushions around its eardrum—and water conducts sound better than air does. The silent world of the fetus (or below the surface of the ocean) is a fantasy, unfounded in reality. To a

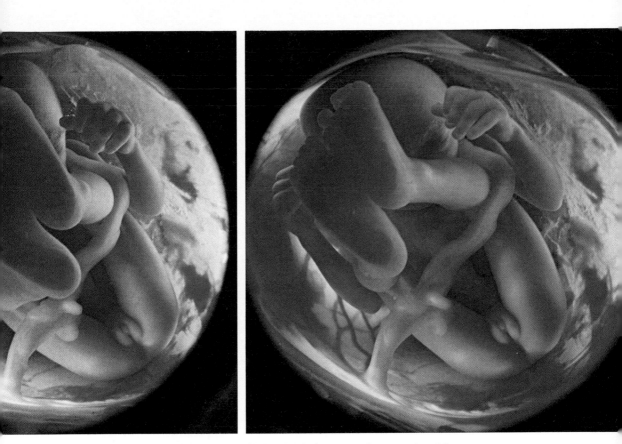

within the amniotic sac. This little girl is just over five months old, and roughly 25 cm (10 inches) long.

great extent the fetus can probably hear the woman's voice, the rumblings of her stomach and the sounds she makes eating and drinking. We also know that it hears sounds outside her body. The cries of brothers and sisters, talk, radio, TV, music, traffic—the fetus hears all this and gets used to noise. It makes sense to protect the fetus or newborn from sudden very loud sounds, but one needn't worry about the wailing in the newborn nursery. And there is no need to be fussy about silence when the baby is going to sleep. A newborn is already used to an environment which is not silent.

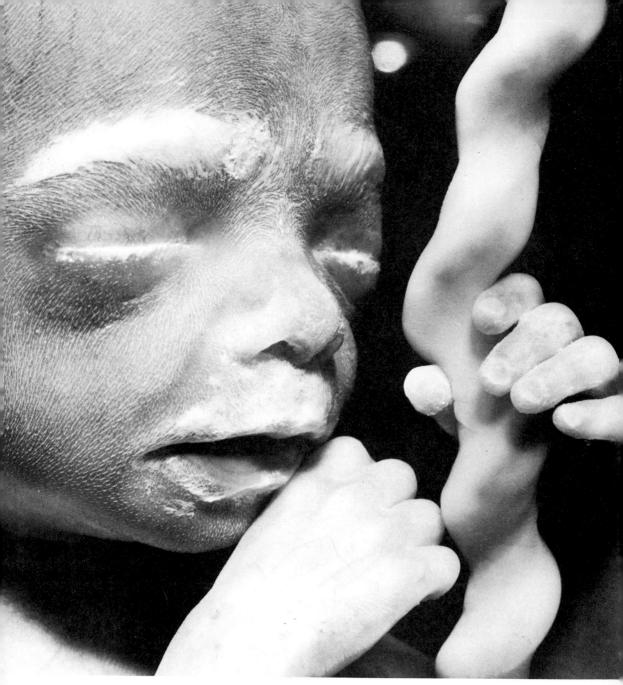

At 5½ months, 30 cm (12 inches)

At 5 months, over 25 cm (over 10 inches) ▶

The umbilical cord

The umbilical cord, grasped by the hand, can withstand rather vigorous squeezing. The two arteries and the vein passing through it are embedded in a firm, gelatinous substance. Because of the pressure from the circulating blood, the covering of the cord (the amnion) is kept tense and will never kink or knot, no matter how much the fetus turns during its swimming exercises. At the time of birth, the cord is usually the same length as the child, about half a meter (1 foot 8 inches).

The reason for the coiling of the umbilical cord is that the vessels have grown longer than the cord itself. Thus, there is no risk of overstretching them.

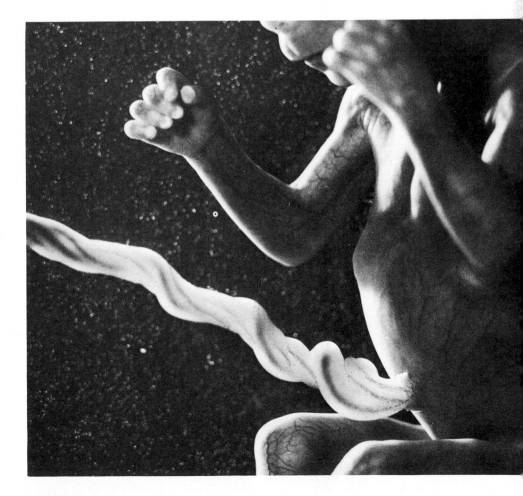

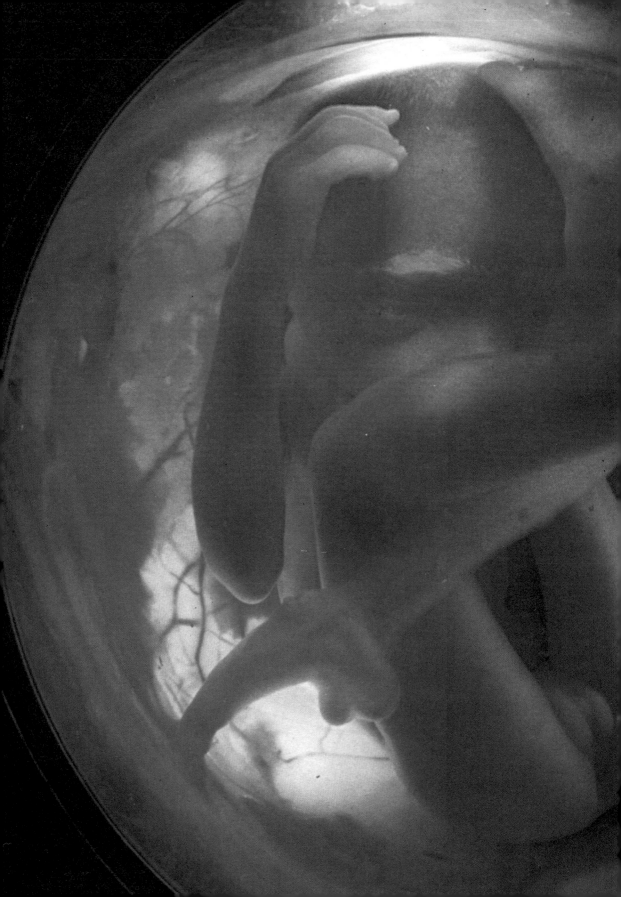

Within the amniotic fluid, the fetus moves and turns around quite a lot. This fluid is constantly being renewed. Besides fetal urine and other waste products— for example, discharged cells from fetus and fetal membranes—it contains substances necessary for the future functioning of the lungs. The fluid also serves as an excellent shock absorber.

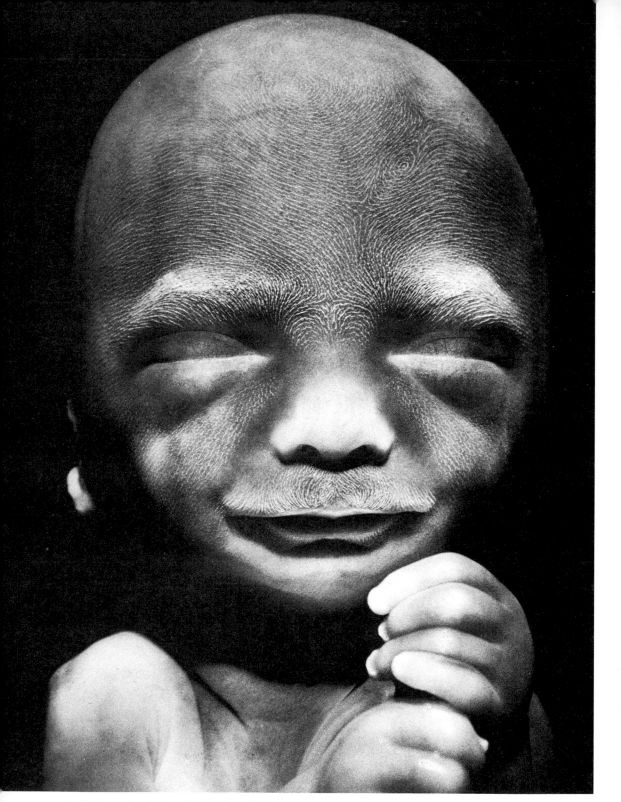

At 4½ months, 25 cm (10 inches). The lanugo follows the whorled pattern of the skin. There is just a faint indication of eyebrows.

Hair

The first signs of hair appear in the beginning of the third month. These are more like whiskers or sensory hairs, which appear on the upper lip, the eyebrows, and—curiously enough—near palms and soles. Later, this hair is replaced by the woolly *lanugo*, which grows all over the body like a downy fell. The hair follicles lie obliquely to the skin and follow the linear pattern of the connective-tissue fibers of the dermis. In the fourth month, eyebrows and hair grow coarser. In children with genes for dark hair, the pigment cells of the hair follicles begin to produce black pigment.

Almost all lanugo is shed before birth. The hair on head, eyebrows, and eyelashes grows rather slowly; the hair style at this early stage looks nicely trimmed.

At 5½ months, 30 cm (12 inches). Coarser, darkly pigmented hair is beginning to replace the lanugo.

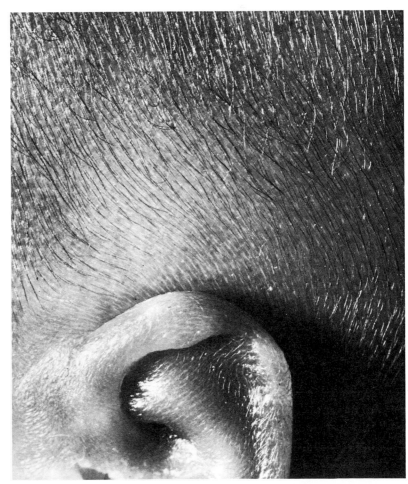

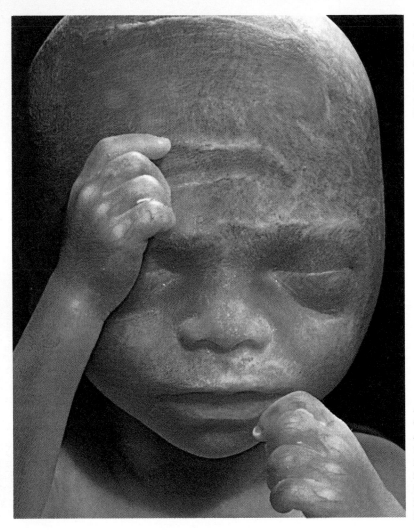

At 5½ months, 30 cm (12 inches). *Left:* The fingers have dug a groove in the fat layer protecting the skin. No chance of scratches—the nails are reassuringly short.

At 4½ months, about 18 cm (just over 7 inches). *Right:* When the thumb comes close to the mouth, the head may turn, and lips and tongue begin their sucking motions—a reflex for survival ▶

Practicing for life

Suck, grasp, and cling—these are the first necessary skills as one enters this world.

Certain reflexes begin during the earliest fetal stage, as soon as the nerves have established connections with the developing muscles. Sucking and grasping reflexes are frequent. The legs kick and the arms wave. These reflexes increase in strength, and the impulse patterns of the nerves are gradually perfected. A thumb for comfort—yes, why not?

The uterus is no silent, peaceful environment. The woman's pulse is constantly pounding; the placenta surges and murmurs; at times the woman moves abruptly, or speaks loudly.

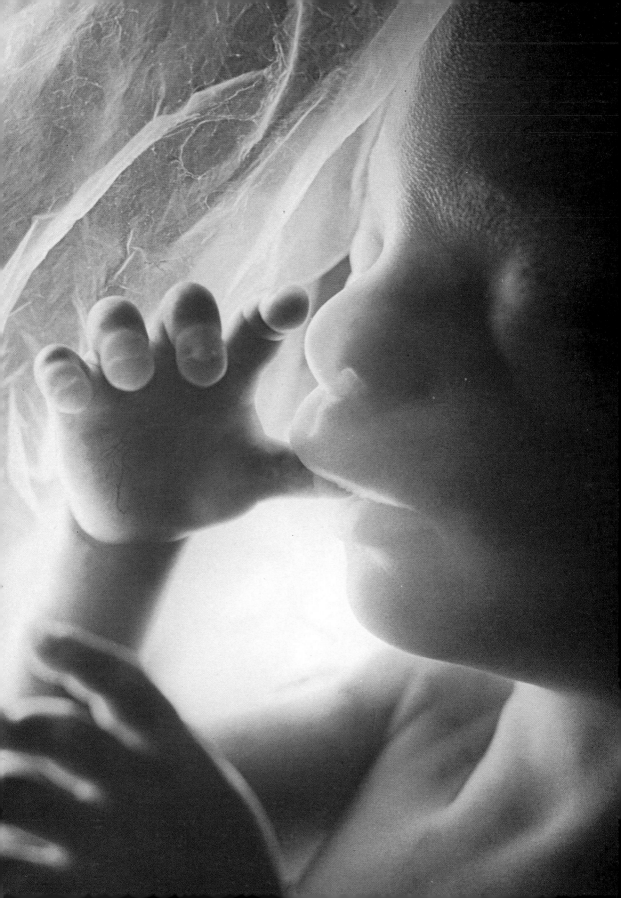

Marks of identity

During the third month, a highly personal pattern begins to form on the hairless skin of palms and soles, the tips of fingers and toes. The dermis begins to elevate in ridges, with grooves between them. These whorled ridges are different on each individual and will last throughout his or her life. Similar patterns in the skin, all over the body, can be seen in the way the hair grows, although they are not as distinct and individual as the fingerprints.

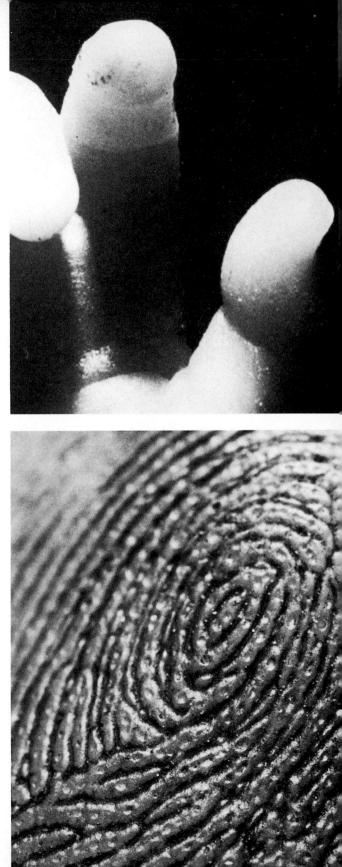

◀ The fingertips may look even and smooth, but the patterns are already irrevocably determined under the surface.

Right: Whorl in the lanugo of the forehead, 4 months.

Left: Close-up of a fingertip whorl in an adult. There are certain principal types of linear pattern, but the details are unique.

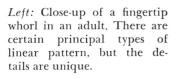

At 5½ months. A typical whorl of hair on the head. ▶

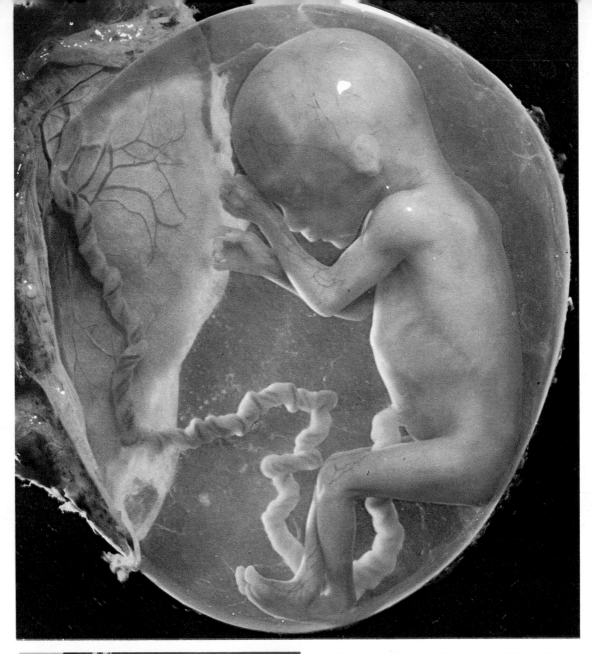

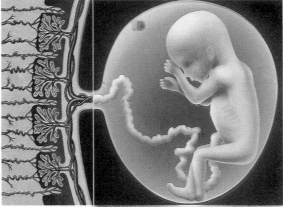

At 16 weeks, 16 cm (6.4 inches). Through the two umbilical arteries, fetal blood is pumped out to the placental root threads, to get rid of carbon dioxide and waste products. At the very tips of the root threads, the blood receives oxygen and nourishment from the fresh arterial blood of the woman, and then starts its journey back. In the umbilical vein the blood is given an additional push, the pulse of the coiled arteries acting like an auxiliary pump.

The placenta—
nourishment and protection

The fully developed placenta is about as large as a soup plate, weighs about 1 pound 2 ounces, and contains almost 100 cubic centimeters (about ½ cup) of fetal blood. It is shaped like a covered basin with partitions, with a rich network of root threads reaching into the uterine lining. The basin fills with arterial blood from the uterine lining and is emptied by large veins. Through the thin cell layer of the finest root threads, carbon dioxide and waste products flow out of the blood circulation of the fetus, while oxygen and nourishment are taken in. This cell layer also serves as a barrier against certain infections and noxious substances. The placenta produces hormones from the time of its formation at implantation and gradually takes over from the corpus luteum, which ceases to contribute after the third month.

The placenta is usually located high up on the uterine wall and does not block the way when the child is to be born. If its location is in doubt, this can be checked with ultrasound or X-ray before the delivery.

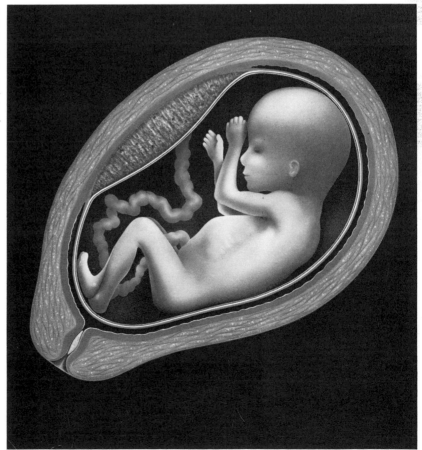

The protective ointment

Each hair has one or several sebaceous glands, which keep the hair as well as the surrounding skin well lubricated. During the fifth month sebum from the sebaceous glands, together with cells discharged from the skin, begins to form a protective skin ointment (called *vernix caseosa* in Latin). The lanugo helps the vernix cling to the skin surface. Especially large amounts of vernix are found in hairy areas like eyebrows, scalp, and upper lip. At the time of delivery, the fetal waters are usually quite muddy with loosened vernix, and the newborn baby looks rather greasy. This grease is a good protection against skin infections.

When their newborn babies are put in their arms, newly delivered mothers all over the world make the same gesture: Gently, perhaps a bit hesitantly, they stroke with their thumb over the baby's greasy skin, and feel the vernix between their fingers for a while; then comes the first maternal caress, with the whole hand.

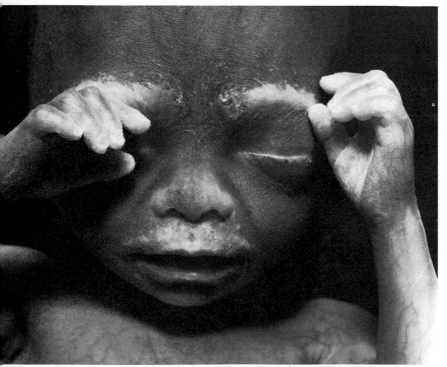

At 5½ months,
30 cm (12 inches)

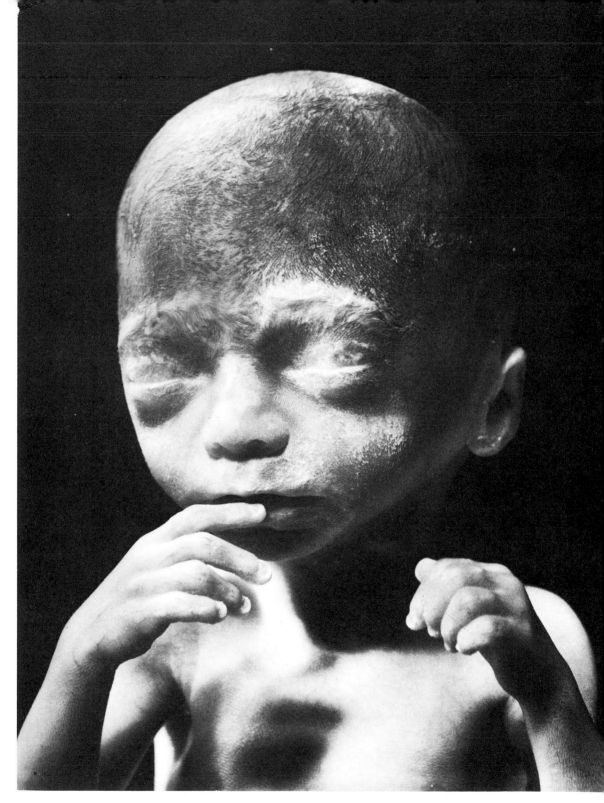

At 5½–6 months

Near the time

The later stage of the pregnancy goes more slowly. The woman begins to long for it all to end and to see her child at last. Even if she keeps working as long as possible, time goes slowly.

The mother-to-be visits the doctor or clinic once a week toward the end. Even when all the test results are good, there may be many complaints. There is pressure; it is difficult to breathe; she gets out of breath easily; heartburn bothers her; her legs are swollen in the evenings, and it is difficult to sleep and turn over in bed. She is in need of a little sympathy. At home, her husband teases her and says she is expecting quintuplets.

It's no wonder that moving around is hard—you cannot be agile when the uterus takes up so much space. The return flow of blood from the legs to the heart is somewhat obstructed. This causes swelling, especially if the woman must stand a great deal. This swelling is not a sign of toxemia. It sometimes helps for the woman to sleep with her legs somewhat elevated, with a pillow under the mattress. The difficulties in breathing are also due to the space getting crowded. An hour's daily rest is what she needs now, and this is also beneficial to the fetus. Circulation will also improve.

Position of the fetus

The doctor now checks the position of the fetus. After the thirty-second or thirty-third week it has grown so large that there is usually no space for it to turn around. If the head comes out first, delivery is easiest both for the mother and the child. If the buttocks come first, it is called a *breech birth,* and the child can still be delivered normally,

Sometimes the mother-to-be gets fed up with her huge, unwieldy stomach. She needs a little encouragement.

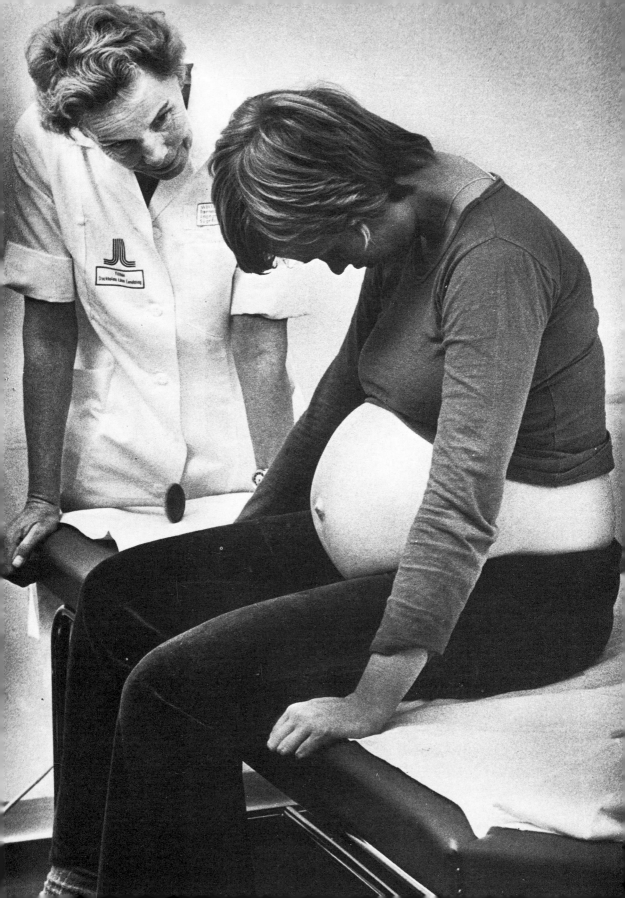

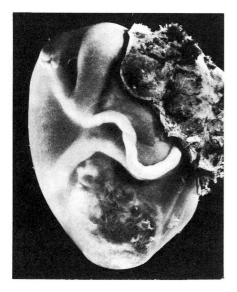

Around the thirty-sixth week the womb becomes quite crowded. Now there are four weeks left. A baby born at this time will probably be healthy, although it is even better, of course, if the child is full-term (forty weeks). Babies born in the sixth month have survived, and those born after the thirty-second week will often manage without special care or complications. Birth weight is no longer the main consideration in judging prematurity. The physician will evaluate how mature the baby is in actual development (respiratory system, digestive system, etc.), in order to plan for special care.

The baby's kicks can now be seen as well as felt. ▶

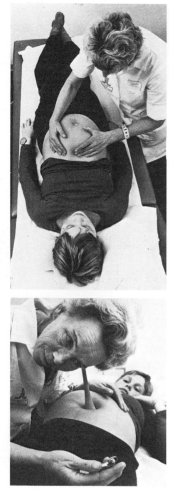

This midwife is gently feeling the position of the fetus. She also listens to the fetal heartbeats. By now the fetus's heart can usually be distinctly heard. When the contractions are strong and regular, delivery is not far away.

provided that the pelvis is not too narrow. If the doctor finds reason to expect complications, a Caesarean section is planned. At this late stage it is easier to determine whether there will be twins. The doctor can usually feel at least three large fetal parts from outside: two heads and one seat, or vice versa. He might also hear fetal heartbeats at two different locations in the uterus, separated by a silent zone.

If the doctor is not certain about the position of the fetus or the number of babies, ultrasound may be used. If this does not yield enough information, he may ask for an X-ray.

Bleeding

The woman should call the doctor immediately if there is any vaginal bleeding. It might be completely harmless: The cervix is soft and filled with blood during late pregnancy, and strain or pressure—for example, during sexual intercourse—can cause bleeding. But bleeding may also mean that something has happened which calls for immediate hospitalization. The placenta may be placed in the front of the fetus, or prematurely separated from the placenta. When uterine contractions begin, there is sometimes a harmless flow of mucus mixed with blood. It is difficult for the woman to determine by herself what the bleeding means, so she should call the doctor or clinic at any time, day or night, if this occurs.

Nausea and itching

Some women feel a little nauseous at times now. Pregnancy puts a strain on the liver and causes these bilious feelings. In such cases she had better keep to a light diet, avoiding fat and hard-to-digest dishes. At times, a rather irritating itching is felt all over the body. This is due to a disturbance of the liver function, and is difficult to cure. (It disappears, of course, when the child is born.) Antihistamine drugs may help.

How soon will the baby come?

All prospective mothers nourish the secret hope that the baby will come a little earlier than the calculated date. The last four weeks are long and hard. The date given by the doctor is a mere calculation based on a statistical average. Two weeks later or two weeks earlier is perfectly normal.

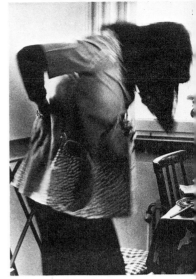

If the delivery is fourteen days overdue, the woman should be in touch with the doctor or clinic. The most common reason is that the date somehow was miscalculated, but in some cases the start of labor is unduly delayed. It may then be necessary to induce the delivery by artificial means. There are many new ways of monitoring the well-being of the fetus. Information obtained from these tests helps to determine whether induction of labor is necessary.

In a woman having her first child, if the head places itself in the pelvic entrance and the whole abdomen seems to drop, this is taken by some doctors as a sign that the child will be born within four weeks.

Uterine contractions—"labor pains"

When the uterus contracts for the child to be born, it is often accompanied by pain, more or less intense in different women. These contractions are therefore referred to as "labor pains," a term which is unnecessarily frightening to many who have not experienced what it really stands for.

The maternity hospital is always prepared, day and night.

Childbirth is hard physical labor. The father can provide comfort and encouragement.

Many women have so-called false pains long before delivery. The uterus actually contracts during the entire pregnancy, more frequently as delivery approaches. In a tired and anemic woman such contractions may at times be uncomfortable. But the contractions of these false pains are different from those of labor proper. They are irregular and seldom painful.

We do not know exactly what causes the contractions to start. When they come, the cervical canal begins to dilate. The protective plug of mucus in the canal is then discharged. This plug has remained in the canal throughout the pregnancy to prevent infections from invading the uterus. It is viscous, and often mixed with blood. Its emergence, accompanied by contractions, is a sign that delivery has begun in earnest.

Sometimes membranes (amniotic sac) rupture before labor begins. The volume of fluid differs—sometimes a flood, sometimes very little. It is then wise to go to the hospital, for the doctor will want to check that the head of the fetus is well positioned in the pelvic passage. There is also a slight chance of infection after the membranes have ruptured.

Off to the hospital

When the contractions are coming on the average every ten minutes, the mother should notify her doctor or midwife. It is time to go to the maternity hospital. In the U.S., a private doctor will notify the hospital. Otherwise, the woman or her husband should call ahead themselves. If the woman is having her first child, the doctor may advise waiting until the contractions are coming every five minutes. It is wise to have a suitcase ready and packed so that nothing is forgotten in the excitement. A dressing gown, toilet articles, perhaps some books or pen and paper might be brought. A nightgown will be useful for the days after delivery. Health-insurance forms (in the United States) and identification should also be taken.

Nowadays it is more common for the father or, in the U.S., occasionally a woman relative or friend to be present for labor and delivery. If the woman has been practicing breathing according to the psychoprophylactic method, she may be accompanied by the person with whom she has been training. All this depends on both the wishes of the individual and the regulations of the hospital, and should be discussed with the doctor or midwife and the hospital long in advance.

Pain relief

Women differ in their need and their desire for pain relief during delivery. Certain complications of delivery make pain relief more necessary. Women delivering a second or later child generally need less medication. But all women should understand and discuss with their doctor the kinds available. The effect of the drugs on the newborn baby is also an important consideration, as we said before.

There are several types of pain relief. Local anesthesia, analgesia, various forms of nerve blocks, and general anesthesia are all used in varying degrees. Tranquilizers may also be administered to women who are unduly anxious.

General anesthesia, usual in surgical operations, means the inhalation of an anesthetic gas, often preceded by an injection into a vein, to produce unconsciousness. The amount of gas can be regulated according to the intensity of pain and the baby's condition.

Local anesthetics are administered directly into the tissue either of the cervix or of the vagina. This is done more commonly in the United States than in England. The *pudendal block* is a common method of pain relief during the final stage of a delivery. The pudendal nerve conducts sensations of pain from the lower parts of the vagina, the urethra, the labia, the area around the rectum, and the perineum (the area between vagina and rectum). This whole area is anesthetized, which offers a considerable relief of pain when the child is born.

It is also possible to anesthetize the nerves leading to the entire region by blocking them at the point where they emerge from the spinal cord canal: an *epidural* or *caudal* block, depending upon the location selected. Such a nerve block may be performed by anesthetists only, and requires close monitoring and supervision. When this method is used, it is very hard for the woman to feel when and how she is to bear down, and she is consequently much less able to assist. To some extent, she can be directed by an attendant. Obstetric forceps may be needed to terminate the

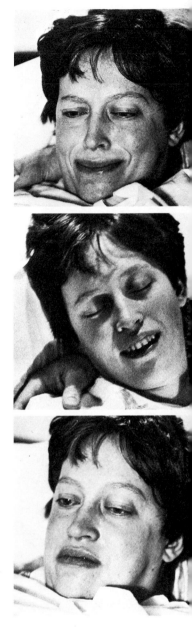

Between each supreme effort is a moment to relax.

139

delivery, or a vacuum extractor may be used; this is a suction device attached to the baby's head.

Delivery

During labor the woman should try to stay up as long as possible, or at least sit in a chair. The pressure of the child against the lower part of the uterus will stimulate the contractions and help with the goal of the contractions: dilation of the cervix.

When lying down, the woman should lie on her side as much as possible. The blood circulation to the child is better than if she is lying on her back.

At each contraction the muscle fibers of the uterine wall tighten around the cavity. The uterus is firmly anchored to the pelvic floor, and all contractions therefore press the child downward, outward. Then there is a pause, necessary for letting fresh blood reach the placenta. The baby's heartbeats, which get a little slower and perhaps even a bit irregular during the strain, return to their normal pace, steady and strong. The woman rests. She must spare her strength until the final stage, when she not only may but should assist by bearing down with all her strength. For the time being she must try to remember everything they told her at the childbirth classes: to breathe with the whole abdomen, not to get tense if it is painful, and to relax between contractions. This is the stage when the father or someone else she trusts and feels safe with can offer great reassurance and comfort.

Soon the baby comes down through the wide-open cervix and appears in the pelvic outlet; one sees it bulging at each contraction. More and more of the baby's crown with its tufts of hair is coming into sight. Now the woman feels like pushing out her whole abdomen. "Come on, just a little more—good girl—push harder—now relax, the contraction is over. Breathe deeply, get plenty of oxygen—here you go, just come on, push again . . ."

No, this won't do any longer, something must happen, she just wants to push and push that big thing which is stuck down there . . . it must get out, out . . .

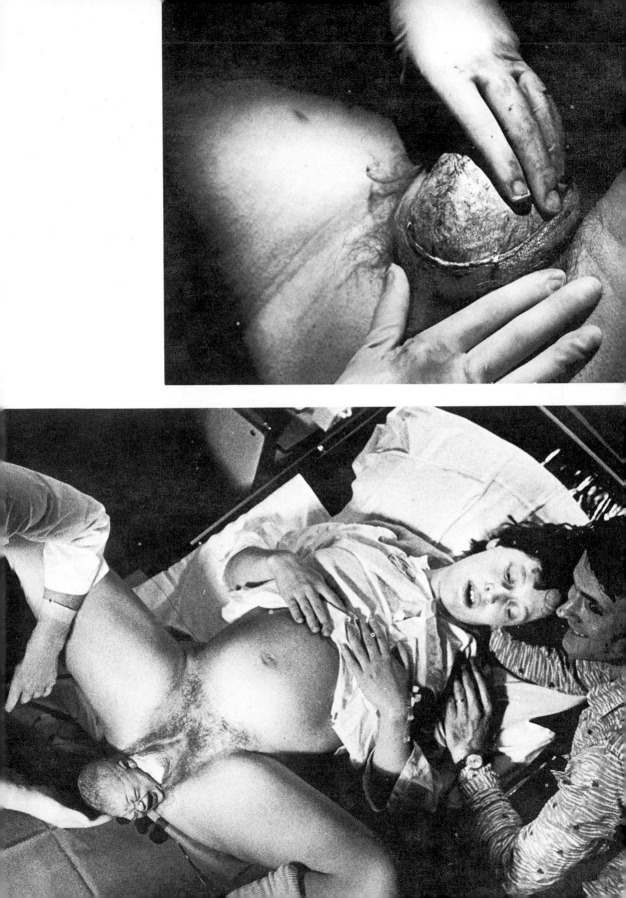

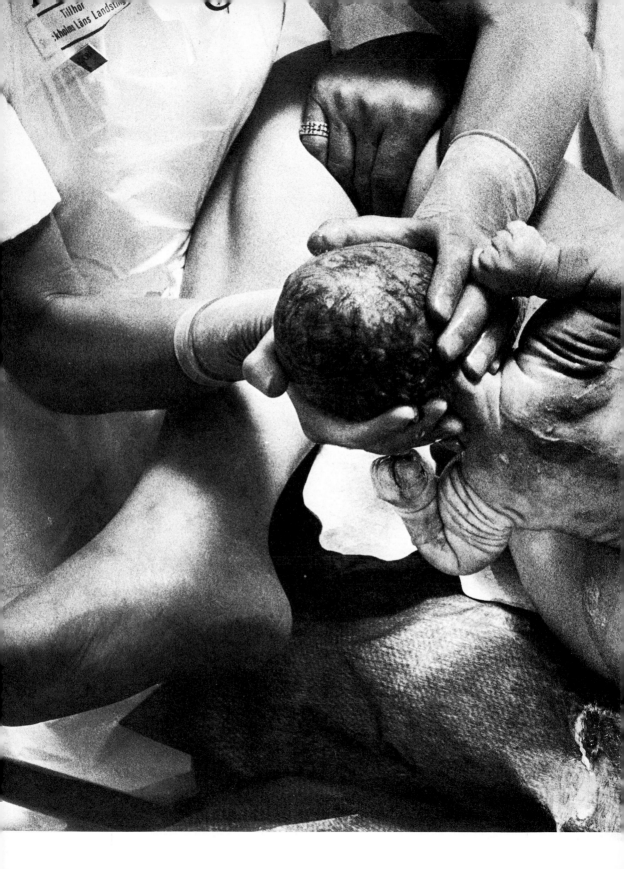

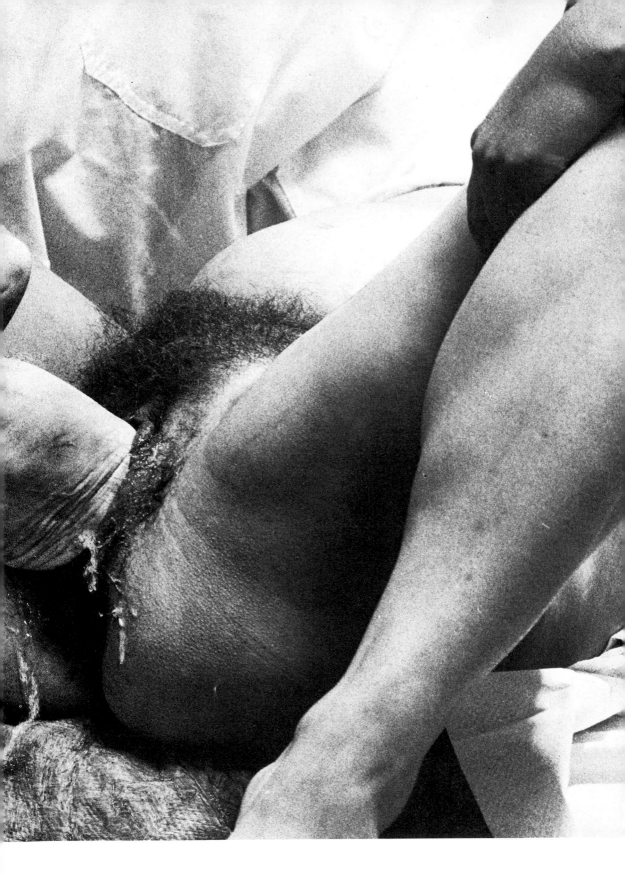

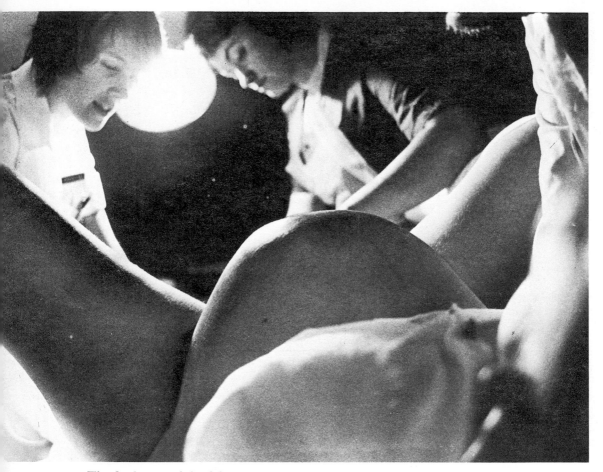

The final stage of the delivery as seen by the mother, just before and just after.

After birth

"It's a girl," says a voice, and the doctor or midwife lifts up a baby girl. The mother looks with joy at the child, which is shown to her down between her legs. At many hospitals the baby is immediately put on the mother's stomach, where it may lie for a while, but not long enough to cool down. At other hospitals the mother will have to be patient. Pain and anxiety are gone now, but one thing remains—the placenta or *afterbirth* must get out. The uterus continues to contract; sometimes the contractions are visible even from outside. A few more pushes, then comes the placenta. It is important that the placenta be intact and that everything come out with it. The afterbirth is therefore carefully examined. The mother may look at it if she wants to.

The child is bathed, measured, and weighed. An indication bracelet is attached both to the mother's and the baby's wrist. In the U.S., drops of silver nitrate are put in the baby's eyes to protect it from gonorrhea, which might cause blindness. A woman can have gonorrhea without being aware of it, but nevertheless the bacteria can infect the child. Tests are being developed to check for the presence of these bacteria, which may make it possible not to administer these drops when mother and child are uninfected.

While the baby is cared for, the mother is also made comfortable. She is washed, given clean bedding, and perhaps transferred to a recovery room, depending on the hospital. The mother may feel a little chilly after the great physical and mental strain of the delivery; she will have

One minute old, after being hastily wiped by the midwife, the baby is placed on the mother's stomach, before the umbilical cord is cut.

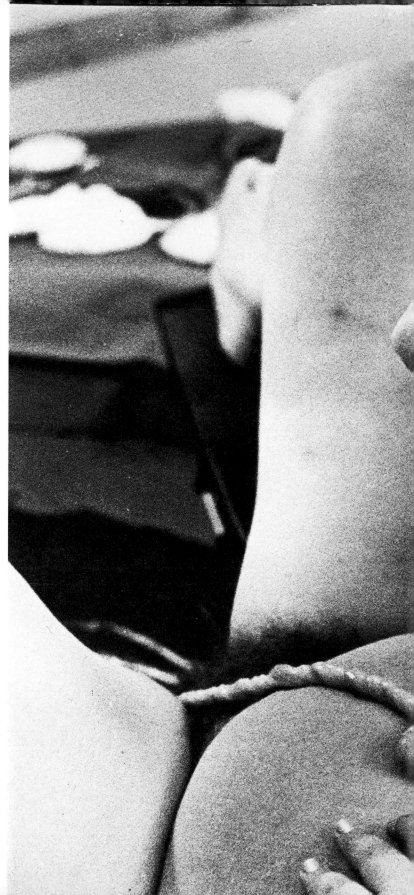

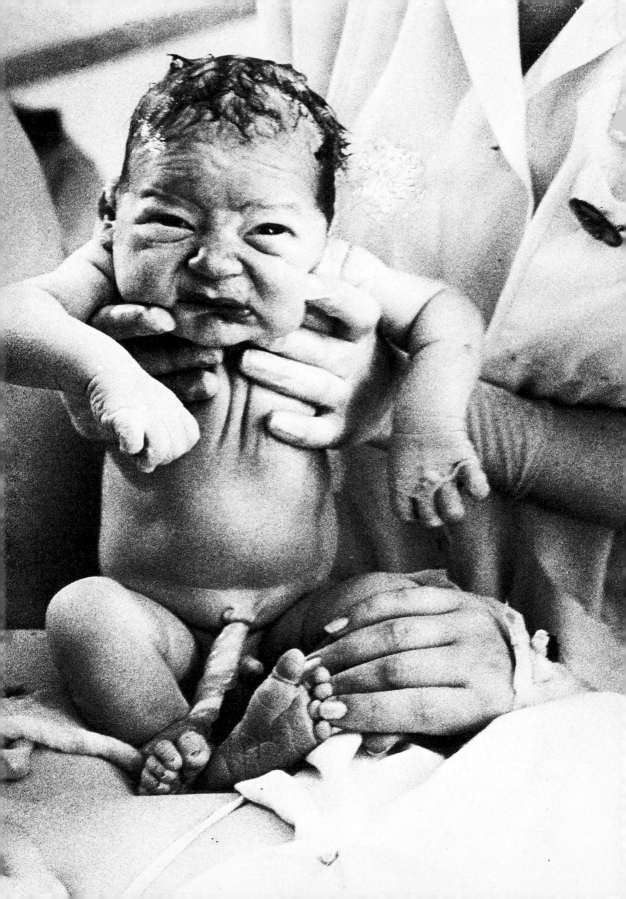

Much care is devoted to the baby when it is just born. More often than not, the pharynx of the child must be cleansed, and mucus is sucked out. The umbilical cord is cut when the blood has stopped pulsating.

The placenta is an important organ which has now done its job. The mother may wish to see what it looks like, together with the fetal membranes: "This is where my baby lived." All this is part of the afterbirth.

The doctor who delivered the child or a pediatrician then examines it. The *fontanel*, the space where the skull bones do not yet meet, is checked. The palate is checked to make sure it is intact (not cleft). Fingers and toes are inspected, as are the hip joints and the backbone.

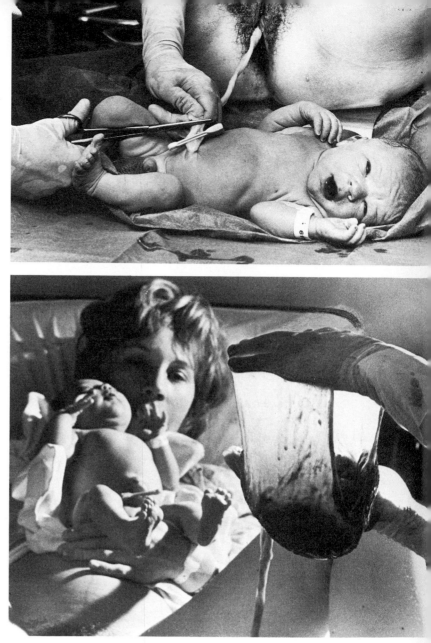

blankets and perhaps a hot drink. While still in the delivery room, the baby is wrapped in a blanket and put beside the mother. Sometimes the baby is allowed to nurse immediately at the mother's breast, which encourages an early feeling of closeness. Mothers should not be surprised if they do not feel instant floods of maternal love. These feelings need time to develop. At this stage, most mothers are happy but tired, relieved that everything went well and the pain is gone. Many want to sleep.

In the delivery room or the recovery room, the nurse or doctor feels the uterus at regular intervals and checks that no after-bleeding occurs. If twins were born, the mother will have to remain under observation for a longer time, as is also the case after a more complicated delivery.

At last the time comes when the mother can move into a real bed. She is brought to her room, usually shared with one or more other new mothers. Depending upon the hospital and the mother's wishes, the baby will either be "rooming-in" with her or be kept in a special newborn nursery. From the hospital's point of view, it is easier to care for newborn babies in a nursery. For the baby the delivery has been a strenuous process, and it has been thrown out into an entirely different environment. The child might have difficulties breathing during the first hours, and signs of heart ailments and other disturbances may occur. All this makes observation necessary. On the other hand, the importance of early contact between mother and infant, and the "bonding" which takes place, is becoming increasingly recognized.

Whether or not the mother chooses "rooming-in," at most hospitals the babies are together with their mothers a lot during the day, for feeding and also so that the mother can learn how to care for them. Nurses carefully show what should be done. Many fathers also want to learn how to handle their babies.

Breast-feeding

About four hours after its birth, or sometimes, as we said above, immediately after delivery, the baby is put to the mother's breast for the first time. There is no milk yet, but there is a substance called *colostrum*, which is also valuable for the baby. When the baby is sucking the nipple, a reflex arises through the mother's hypothalamus, which in turn stimulates the pituitary gland to secrete the milk-producing hormone prolactin. At the same time, another hormone is secreted, oxytocin, which causes the milk ducts in the mammary glands to contract and the milk to be pressed out of them. The oxytocin will also cause the uterus to contract. Considerable amounts of hormones have been circulating in the mother's body during pregnancy. These hormones must now be excreted from the

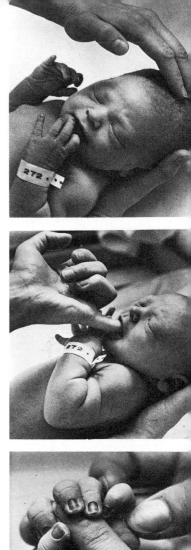
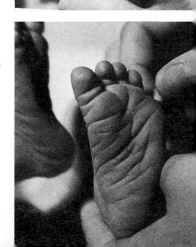

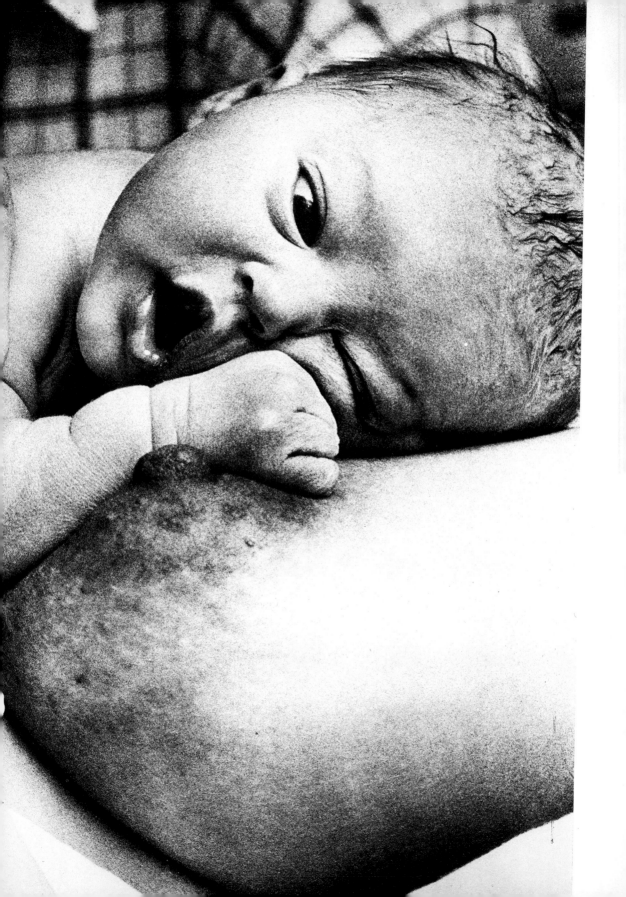

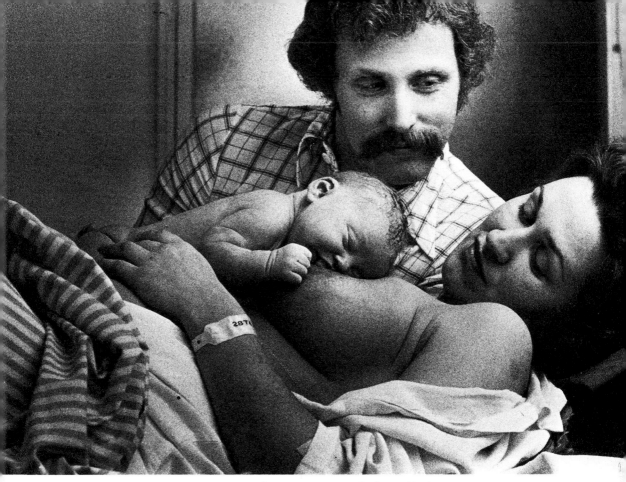

It is good for the baby to lie on mother's naked body, at her breast, immediately after being born. This baby is only eight minutes old, but she is ready to suck, though there is no milk yet.

body before the prolactin can act efficiently and milk begin to flow. This does not come until one to three days after delivery.

When the milk begins to flow, the breasts become firm, tender, and swollen. This is normal. The swelling goes down after a couple of days, when nursing is underway and the breasts have adjusted.

During the entire period of breast-feeding, the nipples should be kept flexible and soft with a lubricating ointment; otherwise, the skin might chap as the baby sucks with its wet mouth. During the first days it might be rather painful for a minute, when the child begins to suck. Soon the nipples get toughened up, and breast-feeding works well. If chapping occurs in the nipples the mother must take great care to prevent infection. The hands should be washed carefully before each nursing period.

There are many advantages to breast-feeding. It creates deep intimacy and bodily contact between mother and child. Those quiet and peaceful moments when the child is lying at the breast sucking cannot be replaced by anything else. Moreover, human milk contains everything the baby needs, including protection against infection. Breast-feeding is also convenient: Everything is ready and in one place. Nature is practical. Some women find that milk comes more slowly when they first return from the hospital. Rest and good nourishment and fluids will usually remedy this. If the mother has any problems breast-feeding, she should consult her doctor, a friend experienced in nursing, or a local representative of the La Leche League.

The baby should have milk from both breasts every time it is fed. It should suck ten minutes on each side at each nursing. This encourages milk production. The mother should rest twenty minutes after nursing, and she should never breast-feed more than twenty minutes at a time, less in the beginning. That would just make her tired, and a tired mother has less milk. If the child needs additions to the mother's milk, one should not give too much. If baby sucks less vigorously at the breast, the breast will not have enough stimulation to produce milk.

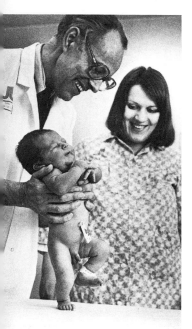

Walking reflexes are apparent right after the baby is born.

Care of the mother

Complications after delivery are rare. Nowadays the mother does not stay in bed for several days, but gets up soon after the delivery. Blood clots are therefore rare. In some hospitals a physiotherapist instructs the mother how to exercise the muscles of the pelvic floor, where they have been distended by the delivery. The squeezing exercise described earlier strengthens the stretched muscles. Slack muscles can cause difficulties later, such as urinary problems or difficulties in sexual intercourse.

During her stay at the hospital, the mother's body is gradually restored toward the appearance and functions it had before pregnancy. The large wound cavity inside the uterus where the placenta was located is now healing. Just as from other wound surfaces, a secretion is discharged. It is first mixed with blood, then becomes brownish and finally yellowish-white. This secretion, called *lochia*, is generally discharged during four to six weeks. During the first few days of this period the mother is very susceptible to infection. Bacteria penetrating into the vagina can spread infection to the uterus and the Fallopian tubes. The urinary passages can also become infected. Meticulous hygiene is important.

Back home

Four to six days after the delivery (about eight in England), the mother is generally allowed to go home. Now she will have to manage without help from nurses and doctors. Life may now be said to begin in earnest. It is exciting, interesting—and new.

At the maternity hospital the mother has learned how to nurse the baby, to handle it, to give it a bath, change its diapers, and feed it. But it is still quite tough for her at home for the first time with a newborn child, who is totally dependent upon her. The baby cries—and it takes some time to learn whether it cries because it is hungry, tired, or has a pain somewhere. The cry means *something;* it is better to do something about it than believe that the baby is crying just to train its lungs. The baby must adapt to its new life outside the uterus. If the mother can be calm and flexible about the feeding schedule at first, she and the baby will find a harmonious routine.

The baby occupies a great deal of the mother's time, but she must see to it that she gets enough rest between breast feedings. She should take good care of herself in order to recover and be able to manage. She can expect to feel her normal self again, entirely recovered, about six weeks to three months after the delivery.

A shower is better than a bath in the beginning. The mother should check with her doctor or the clinic before resuming sexual intercourse. The desire may not come right away, either. If an incision in the perineum (an *episiotomy*) was made during delivery, this will generally take about three weeks to heal. For some women it might

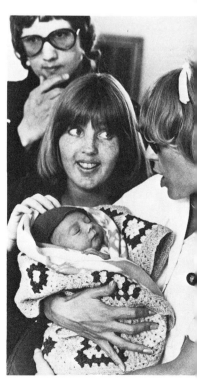

Going home.

When a father helps with the baby, the mother can get more rest.

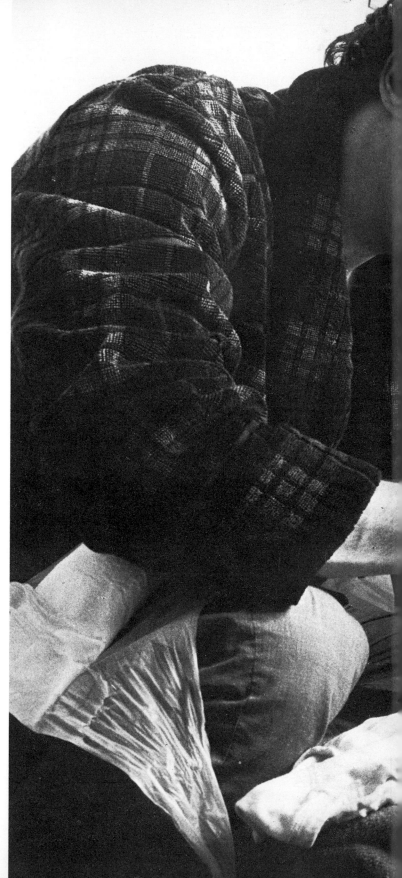

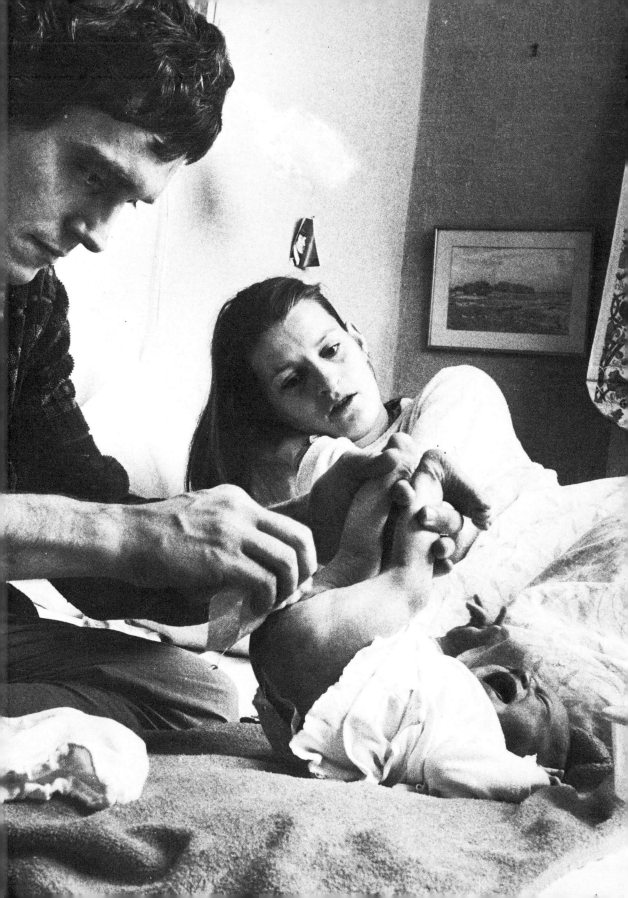

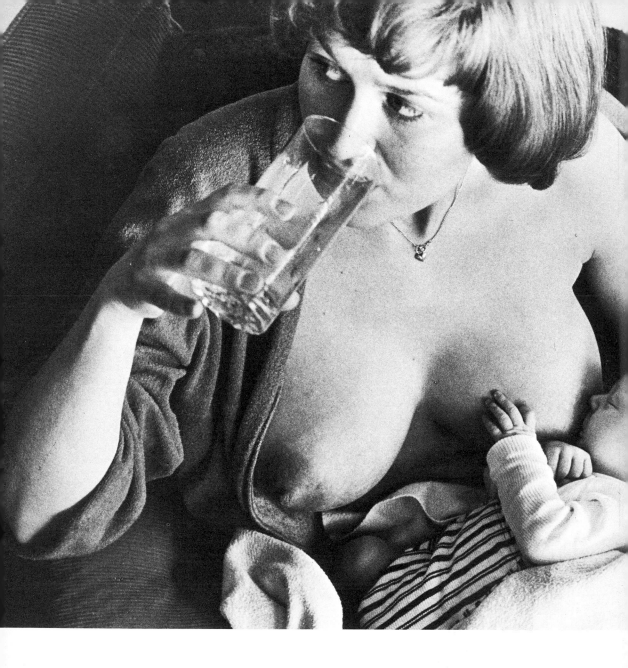

even be painful to sit while the healing goes on. The vaginal mucous membrane may often be thin and fragile; the hormones which make the mucous membrane resistant are secreted only in small quantities during breast-feeding. The exercises for the pelvic muscles taught at the hospital or in childbirth classes should be continued. The muscles should be restored to their previous condition, which may even improve further through training. Varicose veins or hemorrhoids sometimes cause discomfort. These usually subside; if not, a woman should check with her doctor.

Six weeks after the delivery, the new mother visits her doctor or clinic for a postpartum checkup. Suitable contraception is generally discussed at this time. This is a matter which should be thoughtfully considered and not be put off.

Extra fluids help the mother produce enough milk. Sometimes this is supplemented with a bottle or a spoon.

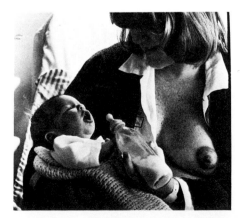

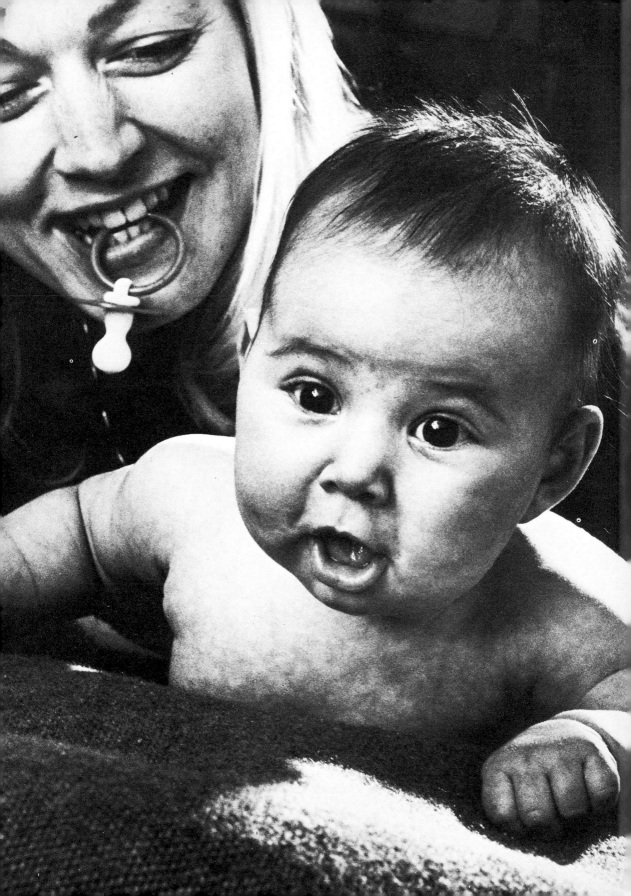

Index